Life in One's Stride

Other Books by Kenneth Hamilton

THE PROTESTANT WAY

THE SYSTEM AND THE GOSPEL

REVOLT AGAINST HEAVEN

GOD IS DEAD: THE ANATOMY OF A SLOGAN

IN SEARCH OF CONTEMPORARY MAN

J. D. SALINGER

JOHN UPDIKE (*with Alice Hamilton*)
   (*The last two titles are essays in the Contemporary Writers in Christian Perspective series*)

WHAT'S NEW IN RELIGION?

Life in One's Stride

A Short Study in Dietrich Bonhoeffer

by

KENNETH HAMILTON

University of Winnipeg
Winnipeg, Manitoba

WILLIAM B. EERDMANS PUBLISHING COMPANY

GRAND RAPIDS, MICHIGAN

To

WILFRED KERR

in friendship

PREFACE

Precious are the disturbers of our peace, those who will not let us live at ease in Zion. Dietrich Bonhoeffer was such a disturber in his lifetime, and he still carries on in the same role though he has been dead for more than twenty years. In spite of all that has been written about him, we are perhaps only just beginning to hear what he had to say. For our perennial temptation is first to ignore those whose words do not echo current clichés, and afterwards to claim them as prophets of the clichés that have sprouted since they stopped speaking—turning them into echoes of the sounds we find most comforting to our prejudices. None of us can escape wholly this kind of illicit annexation of the illustrious dead in order to add prestige to some party line or other. At least, in connection with Bonhoeffer, it is plain by now that his thought is too complex to be fitted into the neat pigeonhole of "secular Christianity." And we flatter ourselves unduly if we imagine that we have only to name ourselves "radical" Christians to place ourselves in his succession. It happens that "radical" was a word for which he had no affection.

The present work is an expanded version of an essay written for the second edition of the symposium *Creative Minds in Contemporary Theology,* edited by Philip Edgcumbe Hughes. It follows the general approach that I adopted in my book *Revolt Against Heaven* and developed in some detail in *What's New in Religion.*

The experience of listening to Bonhoeffer speaking, and of studying those who know his works so well, has been for me a joyful, surprising, and heartening one. I would hope that the present work can communicate something of this experience to the reader, and send him back to Bonhoeffer's writings feeling that perhaps he may not lose the forest for the trees.

Since the *Letters and Papers from Prison* features so prominently in the pages that follow, a word about the text used may be helpful. Reginald Fuller's translation has been on the market since 1953, and is at present the one familiar to most readers. The enlarged, illustrated edition issued by the SCM Press and the Macmillan Company in 1967 will probably supplant it. The translation, revised by Frank Clarke and others, is a careful and exact one, clearing up many ambiguities and some errors. It has also got rid of many colorful phrases—including the one providing the title for my essay—which were paraphrases rather than literal renderings of the German. I confess a fondness for the earlier version, for sometimes a paraphrase is preferable to sticking precisely to the letter; and I have used it throughout. On a few occasions where the new version is decidedly superior on all counts I have added the crucial words of the revised translation, enclosed in brackets.

KENNETH HAMILTON

CONTENTS

1. HIS LIFE

It is the life fully as much as the thought of Dietrich Bonhoeffer that has caught the imagination of men of our age and made him so central a figure in the contemporary theological scene. The commemorative tablet erected in the church at Flossenbürg, the village where he was hanged by the SS at the age of thirty-eight, reads "Dietrich Bonhoeffer, a witness of Jesus Christ among his brethren," and adds simply the place-names and dates of his birth and death. The designation "witness," *martyr,* is the highest title the Church of Jesus Christ can bestow on one of its members. And, although Bonhoeffer did not die directly on behalf of his faith, he died because of his refusal to compromise in taking a path he believed he must take as a follower of his Lord. His commitment to the way of self-sacrifice had been made long before his arrest and imprisonment. It is no wonder that, among the many voices claiming to be heard on account of some special insight their owners possess into the Christian Gospel, even our skeptical and sophisticated generation should pause to listen to one who has proved his right to be considered a servant of the Gospel.

Dietrich Bonhoeffer was born on February 4, 1906, in Breslau, Germany. His father Karl Ludwig Bonhoeffer was an eminent neurologist, and his mother Paula (née von Hase) came from a distinguished family. There were eight children in the Bonhoeffer household, Dietrich and his twin sister Sabine being the sixth and seventh. In 1912 the family moved to Berlin. Karl Bonhoeffer, appointed to the newly founded chair of psychiatry in the University of Berlin, set up house in a suburb favored by members of the university. So there was a maximum of cultural stimulation in the home. However, although there had been churchmen in the von Hase family, the atmosphere within the family circle was agnostic and dominated by scientific interests. Dietrich, indeed, had inherited from his mother a love of music, and at one time it was thought possible that he might make this his career. But when he was sixteen, Dietrich decided to enter the ministry of the Prussian Church.

In 1923 the seventeen-year-old student entered the University of Tübingen, taking classes in theology and philosophy there and also finding time for travel in Italy and North Africa. In 1925 he enrolled at the University of Berlin, and two years later, at twenty-one, obtained his Licentiate in Theology, having completed a dissertation entitled *Sanctorum Communio: A Dogmatic Inquiry into the Sociology of the Church*.[1] He next went to Spain for a year, serving as assistant in a German congregation in Barcelona, and returning to Berlin to finish in 1930 a second dissertation allowing him to qualify as a teacher of theology at the university: *Act and Being: Transcendental Philosophy and Ontology in Systematic Theology*.[2] September 1930 saw him a Sloane Fellow at

---

[1] Title as in London ed.; New York, ed. *The Communion of Saints*. The dissertation first appeared in an abridged edition, subsidized by the author in 1930. A second edition came out in 1954. The English translation is from the third edition (1960); and the material omitted previously, .and placed in the third German edition in an appendix, is restored to the body of the English text.

[2] First ed., 1931. English translation from second ed. (1956).

Union Theological Seminary, New York, experiencing his first exposure to New World society and church life.

In his two dissertations Bonhoeffer can be seen leaving behind the preoccupations of his teachers at Berlin and moving forward to discuss the new issues that were being raised in the "dialectical" theology of Karl Barth and the "existential" and "anthropological" concerns of Rudolf Bultmann and Friedrich Gogarten. Berlin boasted at the time a galaxy of liberal scholars, including Adolf Deissmann, Adolf von Harnack, Karl Holl, Hans Lietzmann, and Reinhold Seeberg. The influence of Ernst Troeltsch, who retired in 1923, was still dominant. Troeltsch's religio-historical approach to Christianity explains the treatment of the "sociology" of the Church in *Sanctorum Communio*, although the dissertation was prepared under the direction of Seeberg and engages with Seeberg's viewpoint rather than with Troeltsch's. Bonhoeffer was to admire all his life the combination of scholarly zeal, broad cultural concern, and personal piety that characterized the liberal teachers under whom he was trained. Harnack, in particular, won his affection. A neighbor as well as a teacher, Harnack seemed to him to typify all that was best in the older generation of scholars. And, when the world-famous historian of dogma died, he read an address on behalf of the students of his generation at the memorial service held on June 15, 1930. In prison thirteen years later, he could still turn back to his old teacher's books with amazement at their author's ability. But, at the same time, he knew that the cultural milieu that had shaped the outlook of nineteenth-century liberalism had disappeared and could not be formative for him and his contemporaries.

As a schoolboy during the First World War, with its bitter aftermath of blockade and the humiliation of the Treaty of Versailles, Bonhoeffer saw the dissolution of the securities of nineteenth-century middle-class life in the German Fatherland. During his stay in America, when he preached for the first time in English, he told how the war had come into his own family, his eldest brother (Karl Friedrich) having been seriously wounded at eighteen, and the next eldest (Walter) having died of wounds at seventeen. He went on to discuss the question of German "guilt" for the war. Though Germany was not alone guilty, he said, guilt there was, and also a lesson to be learned by every German who loved his country passionately, as he himself did. "It seems to me that this is the meaning of the war for Germany: we had to recognize the limits of man and by that means we discovered anew God in his glory and almightiness, in his wrath and his grace."[3] This was the theme that he discovered above all in Karl Barth's "theology of crisis," and he lectured on this theology in 1931 before he returned from America to his homeland.[4] But he had little hope of making his audience understand Barth's essential message. The New World was at that time still firmly wedded to the ideas of progress and the power of human will to remake society, too much so to understand the European who had seen a whole cultural age depart, never to return. Yet, while the lack of any sound theology in the American churches appalled him, their social involvement made a lasting impression on him.

When the summer of 1931 came around, he returned home. A projected voyage by way of India, where he had hoped to clarify his interest in pacifism by seeing something of the non-violence program of Gandhi, did not materialize. Instead, he spent three weeks at Bonn, attending a seminar of Karl Barth's. His one regret at this time

---

[3] *No Rusty Swords*, p. 80.
[4] See *ibid.*, Appendix II, pp. 361-372, for the text of this lecture.

was that he had not been able to have Barth for a teacher, and the first-hand encounter with him was no anticlimax. He found Barth as personally fascinating as he was powerful in print. While never one to follow another slavishly, either in thought or in life, Bonhoeffer acknowledged in Barth a unique source of theological inspiration, an anvil on which the metal of his own thinking must be hammered out. From then on, also, Barth became a personal guide, whose letters counted for much whenever difficult decisions were to be made.

The autumn of 1931 brought him to his position as a teacher and involved him in the practical church work (both local and ecumenical) that was to become the focus of his life when, after Hitler came to power, formal academic life was closed to him. In September he attended meetings of the World Alliance for Promoting International Friendship through the Churches, of which he soon became a secretary. In November he was ordained. As well as attending to his academic duties, he served as chaplain to the Technical High School in Berlin and as leader of a boys' confirmation class in Wedding, a slum area. In this last task he showed his concern for preaching Christ beyond the conventional limits of the Church's life, finding not only that he must interpret the Christian message in terms his religiously disinterested pupils could understand, but also that he had to live alongside them to make his teaching effective.

During 1932 Bonhoeffer's work in connection with the ecumenical movement expanded, taking him to conferences in Britain (London, two conferences), Switzerland (Geneva and Gland), and Czechoslovakia (Westerburg), as well as at home in Berlin. He was busy at the same time with his lectures, including a theological exposition of Genesis 1-3, which was published next year as *Creation and Fall.*[5] His thinking at this period was brought to a focus in a series of lectures on Christology given during the summer semester of 1933.[6] But meanwhile the political situation in the nation had changed rapidly and fatefully. By 1931 the Nazi Party had grown from insignificance to become the strongest force in the German Parliament, and in January 1933 Hindenburg appointed Hitler Chancellor. Bonhoeffer responded immediately by attacking the Nazi "leadership principle" in a radio broadcast on the first of February. His talk was taken off the air part way through. The cutting short of this broadcast by the authorities was prophetic of the future. By being silenced, Bonhoeffer's voice was to carry to the ends of the earth.

However, Bonhoeffer's first concern in opposing the Nazi regime was not political but theological. For him practical Christian action could never be severed from theology. Thus at the 1932 Youth Peace Conference in Czechoslovakia, speaking on the theme of the need for the ecumenical movement to find an undergirding theology, he argued that the Anglo-Saxon view of peace as an intrinsic good could not be supported by Christians, since external peace is other than the peace of Christ's promise to His disciples.[7] So his energies at this time were channeled into a concrete task within his own church. Instead of opposing Nazi power in the secular sphere, he concentrated upon fighting the pressure that Nazi ideology was exerting upon the Church, both externally through state edicts and internally through the influence of the "German Christians." For instance, he had no illusions about

---

[5]English translation from 1937 ed.

[6]These lectures have been reconstructed from students' notes. Title of the New York ed. *Christ the Center,* London ed. *Christology.*

[7]"A Theological Basis for the World Alliance?" in *No Rusty Swords,* pp. 157-173, especially pp. 168-171.

the extent of Hitler's proposals to deal with "the Jewish question." His twin sister Sabine had a Jewish husband. Yet when he spoke out—promptly and fearlessly—against the notorious *Aryan Clauses* of April 1933 he did not protest the government's action but declared the obligation of the Church to refuse to implement it *in order to remain Christ's Church.*[8] His first duty, as he saw it, was to expose and identify heresy within the Christian community. In this task he found a powerful ally in Karl Barth. The end-result was the Barmen *Declaration* of May 1934 and the separation of the Confessional Church from the Reich Church.

In October 1933 Bonhoeffer, having applied for leave of absence from the university, went to London to take charge of two German congregations. Barth strongly disapproved, accusing him of deserting at the moment when his presence was most required to lead the faltering anti-German Christians. But in England, especially through his contact with the bishop of Chichester, G. K. A. Bell, he was able to explain the situation at home and prepare the way for the recognition of the Confessing Church in the ecumenical movement when, officially, the German Christians held all the key positions. In the capacity of leader of the German Youth delegation he attended the ecumenical conference at Fäno, Denmark, July 1934, at which the churches were asked "to refuse to recognize as Christian any church which renounces its universal character."[9]

Once again, Bonhoeffer hoped to visit India. Dr. Bell supplied him with introductions, but meanwhile a call came from home to lead a seminary in Pomerania for the Confessing Church. Located on the Baltic, first at Zingst

[8]"The Church and the Jewish Question," *ibid.,* pp. 221-229.
[9]*Ibid.,* p. 294.

and later at Finkenwalde near Stettin, the school was intended for those who, their formal theological training completed, were preparing for the pastorate. One of Bonhoeffer's students was Eberhard Bethge, who became his assistant and, after his death, was to become his biographer and editor of his writings. In 1936 Bonhoeffer's authority to teach was withdrawn by German officials, and the seminary was closed by order of Himmler in 1937; but it continued underground—many of its students suffering arrest—until 1940. Bonhoeffer also initiated a community within the school, the *Bruderhaus*, where he experimented with a form of Protestant "monasticism," one not bound by the rules of the cloister yet attempting to create a discipline of communal living. His experience during this period is contained in the two books *The Cost of Discipleship*[10] and *Life Together*.[11]

Early in 1936 he and some of his students were invited to visit Sweden and Denmark. At the end of August he and Bethge attended a meeting, held in Switzerland at Chamby, of the Universal Council for Life and Work. This was a preparatory meeting for the World Conference on Church, Community, and State planned for the summer of 1937 at Oxford, England. On leaving Chamby the two friends spent a brief, refreshing vacation in Italy. During February 1937 Bonhoeffer was again at a Life and Work meeting—this time in London. But there were to be no German delegates at all from the Reich Church or Confessing Church at the Conference in July. The year was a hard one for the Confessing Church, for the authorities were now systematically moving to destroy its life. Mar-

---

[10]First published 1937. English translation abridged 1948, complete 1959.

[11]First published 1938. English translation 1954.

tin Niemöller, with whom Bonhoeffer had been in close touch since coming to Pomerania and to whom he dedicated *The Cost of Discipleship,* was arrested on the first of July. In September came the closing of the seminary, and in November, the arrest of twenty-seven of its students. Anti-Jewish measures were being stepped up too. In 1938 Bonhoeffer's sister Sabine and her husband fled as refugees to England. Meanwhile Hitler's annexation of Austria and fomenting of the Czechoslovakian crisis made all Europe afraid.

Anxious about the increasing isolation of the harassed Confessing Church, and foreseeing how it could damage the Church were he to be called to military service and refuse, Bonhoeffer was once more in London in March 1939, consulting with Dr. Bell. The final outcome was that, through the action of Reinhold Niebuhr (who was in Britain that year to give the Gifford Lectures), he was invited by Union Seminary to New York. He left for America in June, but returned before the end of July. With the outbreak of a European war seemingly inevitable, it became clear to him that he could not settle to work apart from those who were carrying on the church struggle at home. He had been invited by Dr. John Baillie to give the Croall Lectures in Edinburgh in October that year, and, though doubtful of being allowed to go, began to prepare material on the subject of "Death in the Christian Message." On September 3 the Second World War began.

Early in 1938 Bonhoeffer had made contact with the political underground seeking to overthrow Hitler. His sister Christine's husband Hans von Dohnanyi, who was in the intelligence service, now recruited him for the Resistance by enrolling him as a civilian agent. By this means he was able to travel throughout Germany and maintain his contacts abroad, while his activities in the Church were almost wholly proscribed. Forbidden to participate in church affairs since 1938, his license to preach was withdrawn in 1940 and he had to report to the police at regular intervals. The following year his books were condemned. Yet he was able to visit Switzerland in 1941, making contact with W. A. Visser 't Hooft. During a journey to Sweden in 1942 he met Dr. Bell and communicated to him the Resistance's terms for a German surrender.[12] The rejection by the British Government of this overture meant that there was no alternative for the underground except the assassination of Hitler—a course Bonhoeffer himself had urged—and the result was the unsuccessful bomb plot of July 20, 1944.

In April 1943 Bonhoeffer and his brother-in-law were arrested at his parents' house, though only on suspicion. Part of the manuscript of an ambitious work, his *Ethics,* which he had been writing during the previous three years, fell into the hands of the Gestapo; but the greater part was successfully hidden and was retrieved and pieced together after the war by Eberhard Bethge.[13] Bonhoeffer was first imprisoned in the Tegel Military Prison, near Berlin. He was treated with special consideration, largely because his mother's cousin was General von Hase, the City Commandant of Berlin. He was able to have books, to write, and to receive parcels from his family. However, the integrity of his character and his active concern for his fellow prisoners made an impression far beyond the accident of his connections, an impression that was acknowledged by all who were brought into contact with him right to his last days. This was the period to which we owe the

---

[12]Dr. Bell's account of the meeting is recorded in *The Contemporary Review,* No. 958 (1945), pp. 203ff.
[13]1949. English translation, 1955.

Letters and Papers from Prison.[14] After the failure of the bomb plot, evidence of his complicity, as well as that of Hans von Dohnanyi, of his brother Klaus, and of his sister Ursula's husband Rudiger Schleicher, was unearthed. That October, he was transferred to the Gestapo prison in Berlin on Prinz Albrecht Strasse. Following the bombing of the prison during an air raid, he was sent to the concentration camp of Büchenwald, then to Schönberg, and finally to Flossenbürg. There he was hanged only a few days before the arrival of the Allies. His brother and his two brothers-in-law were executed around the same time, at the concentration camp at Sachsenhausen.

To the last he exhibited a marvelous courage and compassion. At Schönberg his final act was to conduct a service, preaching on the texts of the day, Isaiah 53:5 and I Peter 1:3. As he was led away to Flossenbürg and execution, he said, "This is the end—for me the beginning of life."

---

[14]Edited by Eberhard Bethge, 1951 (expanded ed., 1955). Title as in London eds., 1953, 1956, 1967, and New York paperback ed., 1962. New York hardcover ed., 1953, entitled *Prisoner for God.*

2. HIS THEOLOGY

The attempt to give any reliable account of Bonhoeffer's theological views presents peculiar difficulties. In the nature of things, some uncertainties must always arise when a writer's life is cut short while he is still feeling his way through current problems that are actively in his mind. There are those, indeed, who believe that Bonhoeffer's theological writings, more especially the fragments of the war years, are too slight to constitute a theology at all. For example, Paul Tillich has been reported as saying, "Everybody is always quoting 'Letters and Papers from Prison.' Bonhoeffer's martyrdom has given him authority—martyrdom always gives psychological authority—but in fact he didn't live long enough for us to know what he really thought."[15] On the other hand, it has been argued that we can clearly trace the course of Bonhoeffer's thinking and see where the earlier theological outlook leads into the last "prison letters" phase, the character of which is unmistakable even though incompletely realized. The debate, in this event, turns upon whether the last phase presages a radical break with the past[16] or is to be understood as an effort to move

[15]Quoted in Ved Mehta, *The New Theologian*, p. 139.
[16]Thus John A. Phillips, who in his *Christ for Us in the Theology of Dietrich Bonhoeffer* speaks (p. 142) of a "revolution in Bonhoeffer's thinking."

forward without repudiating the broad theological base on which previous work had been erected.[17]

In the judgment of the present writer continuity rather than discontinuity is the mark of Bonhoeffer's theology, the contrary impression being largely the result of the fact that, both in Germany and in the English-speaking world, interest in Bonhoeffer sprang initially from his reputation as a courageous opponent of the Nazi tyranny. Curiosity about the psychology of a martyr-hero therefore was a primary motive in turning our attention to the *Letters and Papers from Prison,* with the unfortunate result that not only was the study of his theology begun from the wrong end[18] but also his prison letters themselves were used to justify a current "theology of secularity" having no essential connection with Bonhoeffer's own position and in many respects contradicting it.

There are two statements in the prison letters that are crucial for our understanding of Bonhoeffer's mind. The

---

[17]Thus John D. Godsey, who in his *The Theology of Dietrich Bonhoeffer* raises the issue of continuity or discontinuity, and asserts his conviction (p. 264) "that the last development in Bonhoeffer's theology, while indeed unexpected, does in no sense represent a break with the theology of the former periods but rather a bold consummation of the same." He discusses the various proposals to find a unifying factor in Bonhoeffer's thought, proposed respectively by Eberhard Bethge, Karl Barth, and Gerhard Ebeling, and concludes for his part that continuity resides in Bonhoeffer's Christology. It is interesting to find that Phillips (*op. cit.,* Preface) dismisses Godsey's book as presenting "a descriptive, journalistic, and for the most part uncritical treatment of the subject."

[18]This is the thesis of James Patrick Kelley's article "Bonhoeffer Studies in English: How Theologians Become Popular," *Lexington Theological Quarterly,* Vol. III, No. 1 (Jan. 1968), pp. 12-19.

first is the opening of the letter to Bethge dated April
22, 1944 (pp. 158-159):[19]

> You say my time here will be very important for my
> work, and that you're looking forward to what I shall
> have to tell you later, and to read what I have produced
> so far. —Well, you mustn't expect too much: I have
> certainly learnt a great deal, but I don't think I have ever
> changed very much. There are some who change a lot, but
> many hardly change at all. I don't believe I have ever
> changed very much, except at two periods in my life, the
> first under the first conscious impact of Papa's personality,
> and the second time when I was abroad. I think you are
> very much the same. Self-development is of course an en-
> tirely different matter. Neither of us has had any sudden
> break in our lives. Of course we have deliberately broken
> with a great deal, but that again is an entirely different
> matter. Our present experiences hardly represent a real
> break in the passive sense. In the old days I often used to
> long for such a break, but I think quite differently about it
> today. Continuity with the past is a wonderful gift. St.
> Paul wrote II Timothy 1.3a as well as I Timothy 1.13!

The second is from the letter of June 8, 1944 (p. 194):

> You have asked me so many important questions on the
> subjects that have been occupying me lately, that I should
> be happy if I could answer them all myself. But I'm afraid
> the whole thing is very much in the initial stages. As
> usual, I am led on more by an instinctive feeling for the
> questions which are bound to crop up than by any
> conclusions I have reached already.

These two statements must be taken together. The first
indicates the base from which Bonhoeffer operated: a life
lived in a faith that remains constant. The second has to
do with his attitude of openness that is always ready to
follow a question where it leads, because it does not fear
that receiving fresh insights can possibly overthrow long-

---

[19]Quotations are from the New York paperback ed., 1962.

cherished truths, but rather believes that this will only allow them to be possessed more surely.

His attitude he learned from his liberal teachers, never ceasing to be grateful for the example they set in the matter of respecting at all costs the available evidence and of refusing to trim unpalatable facts in order to make them fit preferred conclusions. But his basic orientation he found in the historic faith of the Christian Church, a faith which he believed nineteenth-century liberalism had turned away from and which was being rediscovered for his own generation—particularly through Karl Barth's theology of the Word of God.

If there is one key that opens the door to his theology more than any other, it is the recognition that at all stages of his career he consciously formed his own concepts with Barth in mind more than any other living theologian. The older thinker served him as admired model, as friendly antagonist (the long-standing opposition between Reformed and Lutheran traditions not being forgotten, though not being absolutized either), and as challenge to serve in his own fashion, for the use of the contemporary Church, what Barth himself calls the "happy science" of theology. While he gladly acknowledged to the end his debt to his teachers at Tübingen and Berlin, they could not help him to struggle with his central concern, namely, the faithful proclamation of the Gospel of Jesus Christ for our own day. Here Barth was his true teacher and guide, remembered from first to last in opposition just as much as in agreement. He did not wish ever to be a Barthian.[20] But equally he never ceased to wish

---

[20]See his caustic remarks (*No Rusty Swords,* p. 120) about the "pundits" at Bonn during his visit to hear Barth lecture, their scent for "thoroughbreds" and their reluctance to welcome him because of his "bastard theological derivation." For Barth himself he expresses only admiration.

to carry forward the theological renascence that he believed Barth to have begun.

GOD, GIVER OF REVELATION

In *Letters and Papers from Prison,* June 8, 1944,
Bonhoeffer outlines (p. 197) the course of theology in
this century, through the breakdown of liberal theology
to the post-liberal attempt "at a completely fresh start"
going back to the Bible and the Reformation. He men-
tions Heim, Althaus, and Tillich, and then adds (p.
198),

> Barth was the first to realize the mistake that all these
> efforts (which were all unintentionally sailing in the
> channel of liberal theology) were making in having as
> their objective the clearing of a space for religion in the
> world or against the world.
> He called the God of Jesus Christ in to the lists against
> religion, *"pneuma* against *sarx."* That was and is his
> greatest service (the second edition of his Epistle to the
> Romans, in spite of all its neo-Kantian shavings). Through
> his later dogmatics, he enabled the Church to effect this
> distinction all along the line.

He goes on to give some pointed criticism of Barth—but
not of this contribution. Here indeed is the place where
his deepest convictions about theology begin.

The God of Jesus Christ against religion. Barth's understanding of the absolute contrast between revelation,
as God's self-disclosure of Himself through His Word, and
religion, as man's attempt to reach God through his own
efforts,[21] is assumed by Bonhoeffer to be the necessary
starting-place for true reflection about the Christian
faith. The biblical categories of "spirit" (*pneuma*), the
sphere of the divine, and "flesh" (*sarx*), the sphere of the

---

[21]See *The Epistle to the Romans* (Oxford, 1933), pp. 49-53,
136-138; *Church Dogmatics* (Edinburgh, 1956), I/2, pp. 280-361.

human, are appealed to in order to show that there can be no way through from man to God. The action of God alone can connect the two spheres. He is known only through His self-revelation.

This theme is as prominent in Bonhoeffer's earliest writings as in his latest. In the two dissertations it is already assumed, and not argued except incidentally in the context of other discussions, since both productions are concerned with aspects of the reception of revelation in the human sphere. Here we come across such typical statements as: "Not religion but revelation, not a religious community but the church: that is what the reality of Jesus Christ means" (*Sanctorum Communio,* p. 112); and, "Revelation is its own donor, without preconditions, and alone has the power to place in reality. From God to reality, not from reality to God, goes the path of theology" (*Act and Being,* p. 89). However, for a direct statement concerning the basic importance of this approach to theology we have to turn to the lecture on the Theology of Crisis he gave in America in 1931, where he knew that his audience thought of theology in a very different way from his—namely, in terms of "religion and ethics." Explaining in his lecture that Barth is to be understood as a theologian and not as a philosopher, he turns aside to generalize in these terms (*No Rusty Swords,* p. 362):

> This at least must be clear, what we intend to be: Christian theologians or philosophers. To be unclear on this point means that we in any case are not Christian theologians. For the Christian theologian must know the proper and stable premise of his whole thinking, which the philosopher does not recognize: the premise of the revelation of God in Christ, or, on the subjective side, faith in this revelation.

For Bonhoeffer there can be no question of any natural theology by means of which, from the human side, the difference between the two spheres can be annulled at any point. During his period as a university teacher this is one issue to which he returns continually, taking issue with a variety of contemporary and historic philosophers and theologians who have believed that there must be a method of establishing the reality of God apart from faith. Against all such claims he insists that the transcendence of God is not to be identified with any idea of transcendence that man can conceive. *Act and Being,* for example, traces two streams of thought attempting to grasp the nature of God's transcendence from the perspective of the human mind: the transcendentalist tradition stemming from Kant, and the idealistic tradition stemming from Hegel's transformation of Kant's critical philosophy. The conclusion is that the two streams, though sharply diverging at the beginning, tend to converge in the end. The first makes God unknowable, a non-objective thing-in-itself. The second pulls God into the reflecting-self which can make God its object. But, in the last resort, both know only the thought that remains in itself and contemplates its own image.

Bonhoeffer's emphasis upon the transcendence of God as being *sui generis* and not to be confused with philosophical concepts of transcendence appears again in the prison letters.

The theological focus of the issue of God's transcendence that "shipwrecks" man's notions of transcendence is presented in the lectures on Christology of 1933. The force of these lectures is well indicated in the title given to the American edition of the English translation— *Christ the Center.* Bonhoeffer begins by asserting that Christ, the Word of God, can neither be approached as a conceivable idea nor be understood apart from worshipping acceptance. This Logos requires that we speak of

Him first by remaining silent, so that we may accept Him by our belief.

> Because of its claim to be *the* discipline *par excellence* and the centre of its sphere, christology stands alone. There is no proof by which it can demonstrate the transcendence of its subject. Its statement that this transcendence, namely the Logos, is a person, a man, is a presupposition and not subject to proof.[22]

The Logos confronts our human logos, our intellect, which strives to grasp all subjects by asking the question "How?" and by proceeding to classify the subject before it. But this subject is an Anti-Logos refusing to be classified. In the presence of the Anti-Logos, then, there is only one question we may ask, namely, "Who are you? Speak!" This is the question of "deposed, distraught reason"—and, equally, the question of faith. Christ alone can give the answer, and He must indeed have already spoken before we ask. "Jesus' testimony to himself stands by itself, self-authenticating. It is the backbone of any theology" (p. 32).

Furthermore, the Incarnate Word questions *us* concerning our ability to stand before Him. He asks who we are that we address Him and yet do not know Him. "The mere fact that man for his part can be questioned like this shows who it is that asks. Only God can ask like this" (p. 34).

Thus revelation creates faith. It cannot be validated by anything outside itself, or by anyone except the God who gives us His living Word in Jesus Christ.

JESUS CHRIST, GOD REVEALED

It is in his christological teaching that Bonhoeffer most thoroughly reflects the Lutheran basis of his thinking.

---

[22]*Christ the Center,* p. 28.

Luther used to insist that it was the part of Christian faith to "see God in the despised man Jesus," and in Bonhoeffer's lectures on Christology this motif is echoed. Bonhoeffer asserts (p. 94) that the heart of Lutheran Christology lies in the theological category of the *genus maiestaticatum,* according to which the predicates of the Godhead are received by the human nature of the man Jesus Christ. Beyond the speculative arguments of Luther himself and their developments by the Lutheran school-men, so he insists, is a commitment in faith to the scriptural witness to the Word made flesh. The intention of the intricate terminology, as distinct from its actual result in the church polemics of the time, was not to elaborate explanations of how incarnation is possible, but to proclaim the reality of the Incarnate One. "The question is no longer, *How* can God be humiliated man? but rather, *Who* is the humiliated God-Man?" (p. 111).

Again, we find that Bonhoeffer never varied throughout his life in his understanding of the significance of the reality and truth who is Jesus the Lord of Christians. In *Christ the Center* we are introduced to the title of Jesus "the man for others," which features in the prison letters. In the lectures the title is given more precisely in the formula "He is *pro me* as pioneer for the others" (p. 48). Lutheran in orientation, Bonhoeffer's Christology is founded specifically upon Chalcedonian orthodoxy, and expounded in conscious opposition to the ancient and modern "heresies" seeking to bend the biblical presentation of the God-man to serve the non-biblical interests of various theories of salvation.

Christ the Center, reconstructed by Bethge from students' notes, is in two parts: "The Present Christ" and "The Historical Christ." (A third part, "The Eternal Christ," was planned but never delivered.) In considering history Bonhoeffer, interestingly enough, takes no account of the distinction in the German language—so heavily insisted upon by Bultmann and others—between *Geschichte* and *Historie*. He is content to point out (pp. 74-76) that historical investigation, dealing in probabilities, by itself cannot establish or refute the claim that Jesus is the Christ. What is crucial for faith is to be able to make the assertion that the Christ of preaching is identical with the Jesus of history; and this is attested in Scripture. After all, we should never feel constrained to raise the issue of the Historical One had we not already encountered the Risen One through the Word of the Bible. So the burden of doubt concerning the historicity of Jesus is bound up with recognizing the Bible to be a book that comes down to us through history. Faith in Jesus Christ as Lord reaches us only when we find God's Word speaking in Scripture. While we remain simply on the historical plane we can meet, at most, evidence of a Christ-cult. (The liberal-humanistic alternative of a "religion of Jesus," focussed on the faith of Jesus in the Father of all men, is no longer a view having any historical backing.) At the same time, the faith that says "Lord" is also a faith looking to the man who lived his life among men in history. We cannot separate the Exalted Christ from the Humiliated Christ.

On the theological level we seek the Lord who is present to us eternally. There have been from the beginning two distortions of the witness of Scripture to the Present Christ, one Greek and the other Hebrew, one seeing a spiritual presence that only touches history and the other seeing a good man elevated out of history to become the Son of God: the docetic and the Ebionite heresies (pp. 78-88). Bonhoeffer believed that the Ebionite heresy hardly survived beyond the Monarchians. Modern views seeming to assert the all-importance of the historical man Jesus are no more than superficially in this tradition. Docetism is the dominant heresy of the modern world, whether in the cult of the historical Jesus or in theories separating the man Jesus from the eternal Christ.

Bonhoeffer located the origin of docetic Christologies in a particular philosophical presupposition to which the saving work of Jesus is made to conform.

> The reason for the constant deflection of ancient christologies into docetism lies in its conception of redemption, in which the nature (essence) and personal character (individuality) of man are differentiated. The abstract doctrine of God and the idea of redemption have the same presupposition, the contrast of idea and phenomenon which we have already mentioned. The idea is substance, the phenomenon is accident; Christ the God is substance, Jesus the man is accident (p. 81).

The result of adopting this viewpoint is (pp. 43-45) that the Present Christ is found either in a supra-temporal influence persisting in the Christian community or else in an ideal character discovered in the picture of the man Jesus by our discernment. In both variants the result is a depersonalizing of the Present Christ. He is present as a power, *dynamis,* and not as a person. This is true, says Bonhoeffer (p. 44), even where the "personality" of Jesus is supposed to reveal His Christhood; for personality is fundamentally an apersonal concept, issuing in the "neuters" *power* and *value.* The Christhood is separated from the man Jesus and lives on as a historical energy or an intuited ideal.

The basic flaw of such Christologies stems, in Bonhoeffer's eyes, from the attempt to begin with an idea of redemption rather than with the person Jesus Christ. "Christology is not soteriology" (p. 37). (Once more, this theme is taken up in the prison letters.) The error of trying to know Christ only through His work began, in the modern period, with Melanchthon, and continued with Schleiermacher and Ritschl; whereas, for Luther, the person interprets the work (pp. 37-38). Doctrinally, there is a fatal omission—the Risen Christ is ignored. "Hidden in the background of this idea of Christ there lies the fact that it does not deal with the resurrection, but only with Jesus up to the cross, with the historical Jesus" (p. 44). This comes about because Jesus is taken simply as the temporal manifestation of an eternal power or value that persists eternally apart from Him. It is not the Risen One, but the historical influence or inspiring example of the dead Jesus that is real for us today. Christ can be thought of like Socrates or Goethe.

> Ritschl and Herrmann put the resurrection on one side, Schleiermacher symbolizes it; in so doing they destroy the church. Paul says: "If Christ has not been raised, your faith is futile and you are still in your sins" (I Cor. 15.17) (p. 45).

Luther, on the other hand, interpreted the presence of Christ in the light of the ascension.

How, then, is the Risen Christ present? Bonhoeffer answers this question in the first place by saying that Christ's is a concealed presence.

> This God-man Jesus Christ is present and contemporaneous in the form of the 'likeness', i.e. in veiled form, as a stumbling block (*scandalon*). This is the central problem of Christology. . . . The offence caused by Jesus Christ is not his incarnation—that indeed is revelation—but his humiliation (p. 46).

This declaration of the *scandalon* by Bonhoeffer points to the christological fact he has insisted upon: that we can never ask "How?" of Christ but must always ask "Who are you?" Christ's presence is concealed, that is, it is not available for inspection and validation. Just as, during His earthly life, Jesus was not seen to be the Messiah, so His presence on earth now is not seen except by faith. To His contemporaries at large the miracles of Jesus were not regarded as signs of His working His Father's works but as evidence of His contact with demonic powers (p. 115). "Even the sinlessness of Jesus is incognito, 'Blessed is he who is not offended in me' (Matt. 11.6)" (p. 113). If the Risen and Ascended Christ is now present in the Church, nevertheless the Church does not look like the community of the redeemed, for it resembles every other religious community.

This is where Bonhoeffer introduces the Lutheran *pro me* motif, quoting Luther, " 'So it is one thing if God is there, and another if he is there for you' (WA 23, 152)" (p. 48). It is not the individual's response to Christ that is here the concern of Bonhoeffer, who was always afraid of the pietistic development in Lutheranism (he often calls it "Methodism"), with its concentration upon the awakening in the single soul of a consciousness of its need of redemption. Such an "existential," personal awareness is included, certainly. But for Bonhoeffer the individual is fully himself only when sharing the life of community—and indeed of humanity. I know that Christ is "for me" when I stand as a Christian in the Church and as a human being with my brethren. Thus Christ's presence *pro me* is stated by him (pp. 48-49) as consisting in (1) being "pioneer, head and firstborn of the brethren who follow him"; (2) standing in their place as the Crucified, with the consequence that "mankind is crucified, dies, and is judged in him"; (3) acting as the new humanity, with the consequence that because "the new humanity is in him, God is gracious towards it in him."

Bonhoeffer's understanding of Christ's presence as being an actual entering into humanity on our behalf is a cosmic vision, and it does not stop with the idea of the salvation of individual souls but presses on to envisage the salvation of all created beings. He writes of the Humiliated One (pp. 112-113), "He entered man's sinful existence past recognition. . . . He was really made sin for us, and crucified as the *peccator pessimus.* . . . As the one who bears our sin, and no one else, he is sinless, holy, eternal, the Lord, the Son of the Father." As such, for him Jesus Christ really can be identified with His Body, the Church, and it too can be seen as the center of history (p. 65). Yet, since the form of Christ's presence in the Church is not yet what it will be when He comes again in glory, we see at present nothing but the Humiliated Christ.

> If Jesus Christ is to be described as God, then we may not speak of this divine essence, of his omnipotence and his omniscience, but we must speak of this weak man among sinners, of his cradle and of his cross. When we consider the Godhead of Jesus, then above all we must speak of his weakness (p. 108).

This is the voice that speaks also in the prison letters, in another context yet to the same purpose. But consideration of that must wait until we have looked at his view of man—selfish and sinning humanity in corrupted community—and at his view of the Church, where man's sin has been taken up into the sinlessness of the Church's Lord.

MAN, THE RECIPIENT OF REVELATION

In his two dissertations Bonhoeffer is at pains to counter the liberal view that man knows what he is apart from God and outside the knowledge of God's revelation. *Communio Sanctorum* argues against idealism the reality of the concrete person existing in time and achieving personal being in the concrete situation of moral responsibility. Says Bonhoeffer (p. 31), "The Christian person arises solely from the absolute distinction between God and man; only from the experience of the barrier does the self-knowledge of the moral person arise." We meet other persons because the concrete person in his concrete life is willed by God. "God, or the Holy Spirit, comes to the concrete Thou, only by his action does the other become a Thou for me, from which my I arises. In other words, every human Thou is an image of the divine Thou" (p. 36).

This technical and abstruse language is continued in *Act and Being*, where it is used in the context of a polemical engagement with contemporary philosophers and theologians. But, if the style is complicated, the root of his argument is simple. A large part of the dissertation is taken up by argument directed to showing how a wide spectrum of contemporary, post-liberal thinkers—from Tillich, through Gogarten and Knittermeyer and Grisebach, to Bultmann—continues to try to find a "thoroughfare via 'ourselves' to knowledge of God" (p. 97). For faith there can be no such path. As Luther says (*Works*, XXIII, 135), God is nearer to me than my existence is; He it is who first discloses my existence to me. So Bonhoeffer comments (p. 96), "It is speaking of God which first enables us to speak truly of ourselves."[23] Revelation does not wait upon our reception of it, but places us in the truth.

But here a problem arises that is to engage Bonhoeffer,

---

[23]Bonhoeffer's inaugural lecture "Man in Contemporary Philosophy and Theology" (July 31, 1930) recapitulates many of the themes of *Act and Being*. In the lecture he opposes the beliefs that seek to find the reality of man in his possibilities (Scheler), in his self-questionings (Heidegger), or in his limitations (Tillich). He then develops the argument that "man understands himself not in reflection upon himself, but in the act of reference to God, i.e. only at the point where he really stands before God" (*No Rusty Swords*, p. 65).

in one form or another, for the rest of his life. So long as he felt that his task was to stand with Barth and assert the primacy of revelation over against idealism's rationalistic imperialism, he could refer everything to God's will. In the *Sanctorum Communio* he could write (p. 31) that idealism had no understanding of the human person because it had "no voluntarist concept of God." But now he faces the question of how interpreting God in terms of will, inevitably leads to stating theology in terms of a transcendentalist philosophy, where God is seen wholly in terms of "act" and never enters the sphere of "being." This means that revelation cannot reveal to us anything about our "being" as persons.

Already in the first dissertation he had crossed swords with Barth in a lengthy footnote (pp. 226-227) on the nature of Christian love, arguing that Barth dissolves the neighbor by saying we love the Unknown One in him rather than loving the person he is in himself. Challenging Barth's statement in his *Romans* (p. 542) that the other man is significant simply as "a parable of the Wholly Other," and "in himself is trivial and temporal," he had asked (p. 227), "Am I ultimately alone in the world with God?" Now in *Act and Being* he takes up the criticism that afterwards was to appear in the *Letters and Papers from Prison* in the often quoted charge contained in the letter of June 8, 1944 (p. 198; my italics), "... *His theology of revelation* becomes positivist, a 'positivism of revelation,' as I put it." The present form of this criticism in *Act and Being* is that Barth's understanding of revelation as God's free act seems to demand a nontemporal movement which cannot involve the historical person, whose response in faith "becomes at most a pointer to God's activity" (pp. 82-83). The man to whom revelation comes is discontinuous with himself if, as

Barth puts it, the man to whom God reveals Himself (*sich offenbart*) is the man to whom God cannot become manifest (*offenbar*) (p. 101). A timeless act cannot have continuity with our being in time. Consequently, Barth "can conceive revelation only as non-revelation" (p. 102).

The alternative Bonhoeffer proposes is to accept Barth's argument that the Word of God cannot be bound and is not "objectively" available to us, but to revise the presentation of revelation in terms of "act" alone.

> In revelation it is a question less of God's freedom on the far side of us, i.e., his eternal isolation and aseity, than of his forth-proceeding, his *given* Word, his bond in which he had bound himself, of his freedom as it is most strongly attested in his having freely bound himself to historical man, having placed himself at man's disposal. God is not free *of* man but *for* man. Christ is the Word of his freedom. God is *there,* which is to say: not in eternal non-objectivity but (looking ahead for the moment) "haveable", graspable in his Word within the Church. Here a substantial comes to supplant the formal understanding of God's freedom. If it should prove itself it will suggest a redirection of the act toward ontological ideas (pp. 90-91).

Naturally, there is no thought in Bonhoeffer's mind of going back to some man-made ontological theory. Seeking what he calls a *genuine* and *theological* ontology, he finds it in revelation conceived as a mode of the being of man, which is also the being of the divine person—the reality of revelation "understood as 'being in Christ' i.e. 'being in the Church' " (p. 115).

Thus man and his existence are not entities we can know in themselves. Only in Christ and in the Church, the community of which Christ is the Living Head, does it become "permissible to speak theologically about the nature of man, his knowledge of God, God's knowledge of him" (p. 116).[24]

THE CHURCH, CHRIST PRESENT IN THE WORLD

The Church is the constant preoccupation of Bonhoeffer's thinking, because of his concern with the "concrete" in our existence. When he chose his career and became an academic, he was also strongly attracted to the pastoral ministry.[25] Events led him into the thick of church politics when the struggle with the German Christians became acute, but he was already deeply engaged in the practical side of the ecumenical movement. In his work at the seminary at Finkenwalde he was directly involved in planning a strategy for churchmen living under battle conditions within a hostile state. Only in his final imprisonment was he forced to live and think in isolation from the Christian community—and still his thoughts were about the future role of the Church in the world!

The *Sanctorum Communio* shows Bonhoeffer beginning his work as a thinker by engaging himself with the meaning of the Christian Gospel for community, anxious to be brought "close to the problem of reality, of the real barrier, and thus of basic social relations" (p. 31). His argument springs from the assumption that the message of Christianity is not about abstractions but about actual

---

[24]Cf. the inaugural lecture "Man in Contemporary Philosophy and Theology": "Therefore man can no longer understand himself from himself, but only from Christ, who exists as community, i.e. from his Word, which the community hears and without which the community does not exist" (*No Rusty Swords,* p. 68).

[25]Cf. his letter to Barth after his arrival in London in October 1933. "I have always very much wanted to become a pastor; I've already told you that a couple of times before" (*No Rusty Swords,* p. 234).

life, not about man in general but about men facing the
practical problems of their existence—about *persons*.
"Concrete personal being arises from the concrete situation" (*ibid*.). And personal being means persons in relation. This is the conviction leading him to attempt "a
dogmatic inquiry into the sociology of the church" (the
subtitle to his dissertation). "In the Christian concept
of God, known to us from the revelation in Christ, but
also from the church of Christ, the community of God
and social community belong together" (p. 40). Thus he
can assert, "The church is the presence of Christ, as
Christ is the presence of God" (p. 101). For that which
makes the Church the Church, namely, the unity of the
preached Word and the sacraments, is the visible restora-
tion of community shattered by sin. Because God's will is
always directed toward "actual historical man," and man
has departed from God, ". . . now God himself must speak
and act, and because his Word is always deed this means
that he simultaneously accomplishes a new creation of
men" (p. 103). Christ has come in history both as the
revelation of God and as the fulfillment of His will for
community.[26]

Bonhoeffer will have no playing with the notion of an
ideal Church divorced from the empirically visible Church.
In *Act and Being* he argues, "The community in question
is concretely visible, is the Christian Church which hears
and believes the preaching of the Word" (p. 125). This
Church is not the institutional "Catholic Church," which
proves to be the "true" Church by pointing to its historical continuity and worldwide extension, but neither is
it a spiritual company composed of individuals who have

---

[26]In *Christ the Center* Bonhoeffer asserts that, because Christ
is the center of history, the Church too must be understood as the
center of history (p. 65).

separately responded to the preaching of the Word and who, added together, compose an invisible fellowship of "true" believers. "It is outside 'me' that the gospel is proclaimed and heard, that Christ 'is' in his community" (p. 123). Consequently, Bonhoeffer says of the Church not only that it is created through the presence of Christ in Word and sacrament, but also that it *prays*. It lives and acts through the faith that it confesses. It is the Body that lives under the control of its Head.

But what then are we to make of the evident fact that the Church is not the conspicuous place where Christ is seen, that it is divided, permeated by godlessness, confused in its utterances, and appears more concerned with its institutional forms than with its obedience to its Lord? Bonhoeffer's reply in *Act and Being* is that the Church can be a "true" community of persons only because it is "Christ-founded." Apart from the Holy Spirit within it, it is a religious community founded by men, and therefore can be observed "hovering between entity and non-entity" (p. 25). In Christ it "is"; but, since it is a community of sinners, it also "is not"—it is a part of the old, disrupted order disobedient to God's will and serving the Old Adam rather than the New. In a paper "What Is the Church?" prepared in 1932 in connection with his Berlin lectures he addresses himself directly to this topic.

> The church is a bit of the world, a lost, godless world, under the curse, a complacent, evil world. And the church is the evil world to the highest degree because, in it, the name of God is misused, because in it God is made a plaything, man's idol. Indeed it is simply the eternally lost, anti-Christian world if it emerges from its ultimate solidarity with the evil world and sets itself up, boasting against the world. But the church is a bit of the qualified world, qualified by God's revealing, gracious Word, which, completely surrendered and handed over to the world, secures the world for God and does not give it up.

> Really in the world, really the presence of God. The
> church is not a consecrated sanctuary, but the world, the
> world called by God to God; therefore there is only *one*
> church in all the world.[27]

This is the Church in its duality, seen from the human
side and from the divine side. He goes on to say that we
miss the point if we think that there are two churches
being spoken of here. "The church is one and the same
with its visible form and in its hidden godliness. Just as
there is one and the same Lord, the carpenter's son from
Nazareth and the Son of God" (p. 155).

Christology is Bonhoeffer's reference whenever he de-
scribes the Church. As Christ's messiahship was hidden
during his earthly life, so the "godward" side of the
Church is hidden except to those who are "within the
communion" of the Humiliated One known by the Body
as the Exalted One. Bonhoeffer ends *Christ the Center*
with a meditation on how the Church can never strive for
a visible confirmation of its way, since its way is to
renounce all claims for itself. It is only good "if the church
humbly acknowledges its sins, allows itself to be forgiven
and acknowledges its Lord" (p. 118). Its visibility is
always in duality. Yet this visibility is what makes it the
Church. The *scandalon* cannot be removed, and nowhere
else can we find Christ.

The Church is visible, a concrete community. It was
this conviction that fired Bonhoeffer as he entered the
"church-struggle" on behalf of the Confessing Church.
Although it was a task he took up reluctantly, once
committed he pursued it with energy and single-minded
intensity. The firm conclusions he reached dismayed even
many who were with him in principle. In a paper "The
Question of the Boundaries of the Church and Church

---

[27]*No Rusty Swords,* pp. 153-154.

Union" printed in *Evangelische Theologie,* June 1936, we find the sharp statement,

> *Extra ecclesiam nulla salus.* The question of church membership is the question of salvation. The boundaries of the church are the boundaries of salvation. Whoever knowingly cuts himself off from the Confessing Church in Germany cuts himself off from salvation.[28]

A little later in the same paper he explains that saying that there is no salvation outside the Church is not a theoretical judgment about who is saved and who is lost but a humble confession that the Church is the only place where the promise of God rests. There is, Bonhoeffer adds, an analogy here with Luther's words about God being everywhere, yet it is not His will that you should look for Him everywhere.[29]

The Confessing Church was to be a disappointment for Bonhoeffer, as he found it turning in upon itself rather than going forward to meet the challenge of the times. The evidence is to be seen in the *Letters and Papers from Prison.* Characteristically, we find him writing on Reformation Day, October 31, 1943, and commenting (p. 71) on how Luther's hopes for the Church and for Western Christendom were brought to nothing. The parallel with his own times is clear. Yet one of his last letters, dated August 10, 1944, concludes (p. 242), equally characteristically, "God does not give us everything we want, but he does fulfil his promises, i.e. he still remains Lord of the earth and still preserves his Church. . . ." Christ's presence in the Church may remain hidden, but the Church cannot cease to be the place where He chooses to be found.

---

[28]*The Way to Freedom,* pp. 93-94.

[29]Cf. the reference to Luther's explanation of the presence of Christ in the sacrament in *Christ the Center,* p. 57.

ETHICS, THE CHRISTIAN IN THE WORLD

For one whose thought begins with the concrete person in the concrete situation, the problem of ethics must immediately present itself. And so it is with Bonhoeffer, whose interest in the subject runs through his life and comes to a peak in the fragments of the *Ethics,* the book he had hoped to make his *magnum opus.*

Already in 1929, in an address given to the congregation at Barcelona, Bonhoeffer lays down the general direction of his ethical thinking. "What Is a Christian Ethic?" begins by separating ethical codes, which are the product of history, from the Christian message, which stands beyond good and evil in its proclamation of the grace of God, since that grace is not bound by men's good or evil works. The Christian message brings no new commandment, in the sense of any moral principle—including the principle of love. Rather, it reminds us that we are not our own and must look continually to God to know His will for us. Led by the Holy Spirit, we find freedom in the decision that must be made in faithfulness to God, and not to rules. The Christian "acts because the will of God seems to bid him to, without a glance at others, at what is usually called morals, and no one but himself and God can know whether he has acted well or badly" (*No Rusty Swords*, p. 44). At the same time, the Christian cannot take ethical decision lightly, as though his conduct were guaranteed to be right because he is in the service of God. Ethics is "a matter of earth and blood," and the Christian "remains earthbound, even when his desire is towards God" (p. 47). Without entering into all the complexities of the earthly situation, and finding how the world never offers us more than the choice between one evil and another, we cannot know how God is always leading us through evil to Himself.

This early address gives us the abiding core of Bonhoeffer's ethical outlook. Just as he cannot think of anyone's faith as being real unless that faith acknowledges
Christ concretely present in the Church, so he cannot
think of anyone as having the right to call himself a
Christian in the presence of others unless he is ethically
involved as a Christian in his concrete situation among
these others. This emphasis, during the period at Finkenwalde, produced the works outlining a strategy of dedicated Christian living: *The Cost of Discipleship* and *Life
Together*. The first book, with its attack upon the preva-
lence in Lutheranism of "cheap grace" (justification by
faith made into a theory to be accepted instead of the
recognition that we belong to God), was one his Lutheran conscience afterwards disapproved of somewhat, because it tended to bend the Christian life too much in the
direction of a cultivation of "holiness." Nevertheless, he
would not go back on it.[30] The conviction remained firm
that there can be no obedience without concrete action,
and that when Christ calls a man He calls him to die:
both in taking the way of suffering from which there is no
turning back, and also in embracing the love of the other
which is a dying to self.[31]

The *Ethics,* as we have it, is a pile of roughly cut
stones. It confirms and develops the stance of the Barcelona address, insisting that Christian ethics must be
neither abstract nor "practical" but concrete. Over against

---

[30]See *Letters and Papers from Prison,* letter of July 21, 1944,
p. 226.

[31]Luther's description of the sinful self as the *cor curvatum in
se* was always a favorite one with Bonhoeffer, and thus the
destruction of the self-enclosed heart becomes for him the proof of
the action of grace. For his description of the two deaths in
Christian life see *The Way to Freedom,* pp. 254-255. The theme of
action paving the way for death is finely stated in his poem
"Stations of the Way to Freedom" prefixed to the *Ethics.*

the slogan of "formation" used by the German Christians it sets the New Testament command to be conformed with the Incarnate One, to be a "new man" in
Christ living "before God." Over against the traditional
Lutheran appeal to "the orders of creation"—which also
had been used, e.g. by Gogarten, to support the German
Christian position—it sets the four "mandates" of labor,
marriage, government, and the Church. These last are not
realities "given" in the order of creation, but are the
means whereby God wills to preserve a fallen creation and
remake it so that "the reality of Christ with us and in our
world" (p. 77) may be fully manifest.

An urgent emphasis running through the *Ethics* is that
of the importance of seeing the whole world as the place
where the will of God is to be obeyed. This theme is
developed in particular within two sections (pp. 55-72)
headed "The Concept of Reality" and "Thinking in Two
Spheres," leading into the section on "The Four Mandates." Bonhoeffer's thesis is that, since Jesus Christ is
the good—reality itself—and through Him alone we know
both God and the world, we cannot think that we can
oppose God to the world or the sacred to the secular. The
fallen world, certainly, has fallen under the sentence of
God and struggles against the reconciling message of the
Church. We must recognize the struggle for what it is,
yet we must remember one thing more about the world in
its rebellion. "In this way it is also, and indeed especially,
the lost and sentenced world that is incessantly drawn
into the event of Christ" (p. 71).

The *Letters and Papers from Prison,* from the point of
view of Bonhoeffer's theological teaching, is significant in
that it shows us the thinker wrestling with the way in
which the "lost and sentenced world" is to be brought
into touch with the reconciliation known in the Church.
Much of the debate that has arisen around the interpre-

tation of the new phrases appearing in the prison letters—
"religionless Christianity," "man's coming of age,"
"worldly existence"—is beside the point; for it assumes
that Bonhoeffer was trying to work out some philosophy
of history requiring us to adapt the Christian Gospel to
the self-understanding of the modern age, whereas he
continued to reject strenuously this illusion of idealistic
thinking (March 9, 1944, pp. 144-145). What he did
believe is that we must accept "the facts and achieve-
ments of any given period" realistically as telling us where
men are, since this is the place where they have to be
reached with the Christian Gospel. Just now, he suggested (April 30, 1944, p. 162), we are "proceeding to
a time of no religion at all" and our problem is to find
how Christ can become the Lord even of those with no
religion. So—

> . . . In what way are we in a religionless and secular sense
> Christians, in what way are we the *Ekklesia*, "those who
> are called forth," not conceiving of ourselves religiously as
> specially favoured, but as wholly belonging to the world
> (p. 164)?

One answer he suggests is located in the distinction
(developed in the *Ethics*) between the penultimate and
the ultimate, between the things before the last, which
the world is conscious of, and the last things, which are
gathered up in God's justification of sinners. To maintain
a hold upon the last things will require a "secret discipline" where, in a world that has forgotten the meaning
of "inwardness," the Christian must strengthen his hold
upon the ultimate reality of faith.

But, by the very nature of his unnaturally isolated situation, Bonhoeffer mostly asks questions without giving
answers.

One thing the *Letters and Papers from Prison* makes
quite plain. There is no alteration in his basic theology, as

there is none in his beliefs. He is as insistent as ever that revelation establishes reality, that the New Testament is not a mythological garbing of universal truth, and that the penultimate exists from and is supported by the ultimate. "How can men endure earthly tensions if they know nothing of the tension between earth and heaven?" (April 11, 1944, p. 157). Equally, he is confident that accepting without reservation the relative goodness of the world does not endanger our grasp upon the Gospel. ". . . God requires that we should love him eternally with our whole hearts, yet not so as to compromise or diminish our earthly affections, but as a kind of *cantus firmus* to which the other melodies of life provide the counterpoint" (May 20, 1944, p. 175). Thus he has no scruples about asking questions that seem to endanger the security of faith, or in suggesting that the religious "garment" in which the Christian message has been wrapped to date may be discarded without losing the substance of the message. In particular, he believes that tying the Gospel to any one apologetic is self-defeating. "Religionless" man is not necessarily more impervious to the call of Christ than "religious" man. "The world's coming of age is then no longer an occasion for polemics and apologetics, but it is really better understood than it understands itself, namely on the basis of the Gospel, and in the light of Christ" (June 8, 1944, p. 200).

Sending the outline of his proposed new book on Christianity in the modern age, Bonhoeffer writes to Bethge: "The Church must get out of her stagnation. We must move out again into the open air of intellectual discussion with the world, and risk shocking people if we are to cut any ice" (August 3, 1944, p. 235). He speaks of the excitement of intellectual discovery. Yet he knows that theological analysis is fallible and impermanent, while the Gospel is always the same. "The God of Jesus Christ has nothing to do with all that we, in our human way, think he can and ought to do. . . . One thing is certain: we must always live close to the presence of God. . . . We can claim nothing for ourselves, and yet we may pray for everything" (August 21, 1944, p. 243).

At the end of the letter where these words are written, another thought strikes him (about the sins of weakness). He makes some observations, and concludes, "I must ponder further on this" (p. 244). This is typical of his method—to strike out in thought and then to think it through in relation to the central point of the Gospel: Jesus Christ and the redemption that comes through Him. *Letters and Papers from Prison* gives us only dislocated theological jottings, requiring much pondering and restatement. But it is a true testament to Bonhoeffer the adventurous theologian, whose theology was always rooted in the concrete situation of a life lived in faith.

3. ISSUES OF HIS THEOLOGY

GOD AND REVELATION

Bonhoeffer's conception of the nature and task of theology is outlined in the lecture "The Theology of Crisis" he gave in New York in 1931.

> The deepest antinomy seems to me to be the antinomy between pure act and reflection—as the old dogmatics said, *actus directus* and *reflexus*. God is known only in the pure act of referring to God. Theology and philosophy are executed in reflection, into which God does not enter. Philosophy essentially remains in reflection; man knows himself and God only in reflection. Theology at least knows of an act of God, which tears man out of this reflection in an *actus directus* towards God. Here man knows himself and God not by looking into himself, but by looking into the Word of God, which tells him he is a sinner and justified, which he never could understand before. So as Luther said: *pecca fortiter, sed crede fortius,* Barth could say: *reflecte fortiter, sed crede fortius.*[32]

Although this is an early statement, it remains in its essential affirmation true for the mature Bonhoeffer also.

---

[32]*No Rusty Swords,* p. 372. Cf. Bonhoeffer's inaugural lecture (1930) "Man in Contemporary Philosophy and Theology," where a very similar terminology is used (*No Rusty Swords,* pp. 50-69; especially pp. 64-66). In *Act and Being* (p. 175) he even finds in Barth himself the "danger" of locating the act of belief in "reflexion."

However strongly he might disagree with Barth in other places, he never departed from his theology of the Word of God, and, on this account, continued to call himself a "modern" theologian.[33] His decisive break with liberalism came through his rejection of his teacher Seeberg's notion of a "religious a priori,"[34] and from that time on he was to reject outright any kind of natural theology.[35] On the basis of Barth's setting "spirit" against "flesh," revelation against religion, he distinguished also "epistemological transcendence" from the transcendence of the Living God—a distinction found in his latest writings as in his earliest.[36]

Our estimate of Bonhoeffer's teaching about God and revelation, therefore, will depend upon our estimate of the Barthian "revolution" in theology that cuts the link between human reason and divine revelation. Yet, on this ground, Bonhoeffer believed that Barth was no innovator, and he himself appealed here to the teaching of Luther.[37] Where he went on to criticize Barth, he attacked Barth at the point of his "Kantian trimmings," which seemed to make the Word of God so (epistemologically) transcendent that it could not be found concretely in time, where man lives. Bon-

---

[33]See *Letters and Papers from Prison*, August 3, 1944, p. 235.

[34]See *Act and Being*, pp. 44-48.

[35]Cf. his criticism of American theology: "American theology and the American church as a whole have never been able to understand the meaning of 'criticism' by the Word of God and all that signifies. . . . A symptom of this is the general adherence to natural theology" (*No Rusty Swords*, p. 117). Referring to the *Christian Century* articles "How my mind has changed in the last decade," he remarked of the contributors, "And *all*, finally, are united in deliberate rejection of Barth's criticism of natural theology" (*ibid.*, p. 115).

[36]See *Sanctorum Communio*, p. 33; *Act and Being*, p. 69; *Letters and Papers from Prison*, April 30, 1944, pp. 165-166; "Outline for a Book," in *Letters*, pp. 237-238.

[37]*No Rusty Swords*, p. 362; *Act and Being*, p. 47.

hoeffer's solution, namely, that God's Word is the Incarnate Word that lives in the Church as community, is one that raises its own problems. At the moment, however, we may turn to two aspects of the doctrine of God and revelation that have not received extended treatment from Bonhoeffer: the Holy Spirit and the Scriptures.

The Holy Spirit is most fully discussed in the *Sanctorum Communio*. There it is stressed that God reveals Himself as the Holy Spirit in order to build up His Church (p. 104).[38] Christ and the Spirit are inseparably connected; for "the Holy Spirit has no other content than the fact of Christ," and Christ "participates in the actual building of the church in time . . . only in the action of the Holy Spirit" (p. 116). The Spirit, being for us "solely the Spirit of the church" (p. 115), makes all individualistic notions of faith impossible. Certainly, each individual is moved according to his own election in Christ, but already as a member of the communion of Christ. "God sees the church of Christ and the individual in one act" (p. 118), which is the act of the Spirit's gift of faith to the individual and His building up of the Church. Thus the doctrine of predestination is grounded in the doctrine of the Spirit, the Personal Spirit of the community of persons.

It is the Holy Spirit, too, who inspires the record of Scripture. "The Bible is the Word only in the church" (p. 161). Both preaching and the Scriptures remain the

---

[38]Cf. the entry in the catechism prepared by Bonhoeffer, in collaboration with Franz Hildebrandt, for the confirmation class at Wedding: "*Who is the Holy Spirit?* No spirit of the world, but the Spirit of God and Christ, who is present in the church. Without him we would know nothing of Christ, just as without Christ we would know nothing of God. In him the Godhead fulfils itself on earth for 'if thou didst not have a church, thou wouldest not be God' (Luther)" (*No Rusty Swords,* p. 147).

word of man so long as they are not inspired by the Spirit. "The Spirit has not united himself in substance with the word of the Bible" (*ibid.*).

On this basis, Bonhoeffer accepts without question the validity of a critical approach to the Bible. At the same time he insists that the Bible is the place where the self-attestation of Jesus is handed down to us. In *Christ the Center* he links the question of the exegesis of Scripture with the question of the recognition of Christ in the Jesus of history through faith in the Resurrection.

> . . . Verbal inspiration is a bad surrogate for the resurrection. It means the denial of the sole presence of the Risen One. It eternalizes history instead of seeing and recognizing history in the light of God's eternity. It fails in the attempt to level the difficult ground. The Bible also remains a book among books. We must be ready to admit the concealment in history and thus accept the course of historical criticism. But the Risen One encounters us right through the Bible with all its flaws. We must enter the straits of historical criticism. Its importance is not absolute, but at the same time it is not a matter of indifference. In fact it never leads to a weakening of faith but rather to its strengthening, as concealment in history is part of Christ's humiliation (p. 76).

However, in his own exegetical works (which were strongly influenced by his old teacher at Tübingen, Adolf Schlatter) he made practically no use of biblical criticism. In the Introduction to *Creation and Fall* (1933), based on his lectures of the previous winter semester on the first three chapters of Genesis, he insists that in the Church it is "theological interpretation" that matters. Historical considerations cannot control the exegesis, since the One God here is speaking to His Church.

In all these statements, there is a full consistency in Bonhoeffer's understanding of the "objectivity" of God's revelation of Himself. With Barth, he agrees that God's Word is never bound to man's vision, and cannot be tested by human standards of what is counted to be objectively given. Only faith *knows*. Yet he goes beyond Barth in believing that Christ "is" in the Church, and so he finds that the Holy Spirit speaks directly to us in the Church through the words of the Bible. Lecturing on "The Church Is Dead", in 1932 at the Conference at Gland, Switzerland, he said, ". . . Has it not become terrifyingly clear again and again . . . that we are no longer obedient to the Bible? We are more fond of our own thoughts than of the thoughts of the Bible. We no longer read the Bible seriously, we no longer read it against ourselves, but for ourselves" (*No Rusty Swords,* p. 185).

CHRIST AND THE CHURCH

Since Bonhoeffer puts the whole "concreteness" of the Gospel into the presence of the Risen Christ in His Church, our ability to know where the Church of Jesus Christ is becomes of central importance for our salvation— and the salvation of the world. Ruled out is the supposition that the Church as an institution can stand as the embodiment of Christ in the world, or that the world is to be brought to perfection under the guidance of the Church. In the lecture "The Church Is Dead" Bonhoeffer insists upon this truth.

> No visible city of God is erected in this world, it would not be even if there were international understanding everywhere; everything which the church does here is transitory, it is only intended to hold together the collapsing orders of the world, to preserve it from falling back into chaos. This action of the church is indispensable, but the new order, society, community is not the order of the kingdom. All orders and all

communities of the world will have to perish when God
creates his world anew and the Lord Christ comes again
to judge the old world and build the new.[39]

In the same year as this lecture he wrote also "Thy
Kingdom Come: The Prayer of the Church for God's
Kingdom on Earth," in which he pointed out that Christians can cease to believe in God's Kingdom in two ways:
by adopting an other-worldly stance, which places God's
rule entirely in the hereafter, and by adopting a "pious
secularism" by means of which we seek to build the Kingdom as an earthly Utopia. The prayer for the coming of
the Kingdom upon earth cannot be prayed either by pious
individualist or by fanatical utopianist.

> Rather, this prayer is prayed solely by the congregation of
> the children of the earth, who refuse to separate
> themselves from the world and who have no special
> proposals to offer for its improvement. . . . Here at the
> very center of this dying, disrupted, and desirous world
> something becomes evident to those who can believe—
> believe in the resurrection of Jesus Christ. Here the
> absolute miracle has occurred. . . . Here the kingdom of
> God itself comes to us on earth, comes to our world.[40]

We must notice how another element is now brought
into the picture of Christ present in the Church. It is the
element of Christ's presence in the believing Church publishing the news that God's Kingdom is already present in
the world—Christ present as the first-fruits of the New
Creation. This means that the "place" of the Church in
the world remains no longer of first importance. Instead,
the accent is laid upon the recognition by members of the
Christian community of the witness to be made in the
world to the "miracle" of God's act of redeeming His

[39]*No Rusty Swords,* p. 188.
[40]J. D. Godsey, *Preface to Bonhoeffer,* p. 36.

fallen creation. This seems to join together, in prospect, Bonhoeffer's early concern for the Church to understand itself as community, the concern of his "middle period" for costly Christian discipleship, and the final concern for "worldly" holiness.

"Thy Kingdom Come" states that the Kingdom of God appears on earth in two forms, divided into Church and "the order we call the state." "The kingdom of God exists in our world exclusively in the duality of church and state. Each is necessarily related to the other; neither exists for itself. Every attempt of the one to take control of the other disregards this relationship of the kingdom of God on earth" (*ibid.*, p. 40). *Christ the Center* also speaks (p. 65) of Christ as being present to us in the double form of Church and state—the Church being the hidden center of the state. The discussion of "Thinking in Terms of Two Spheres" in the *Ethics,* with its strong condemnation of dualistic thinking of separated "spaces" comprising the Church and the world, might be imagined to show a shift in viewpoint. Yet, the *Ethics* simply underlines the earlier insistence upon the duality of forms under which the Kingdom "attests itself." Error enters into this way of thinking only where the "spaces" of world and Church are conceived statically and made to exclude each other, as though the "reality" of the world were outside the "reality" of Christ. Thus the *Ethics* asserts (p. 65),

> The unity of the reality of God and of the world, which has been accomplished in Christ, is repeated, or, more exactly, is realized, ever afresh in the life of men. And yet what is Christian is not identical with what is of the world. The natural is not identical with the supernatural or the revelational with the rational. But between the two spheres is in each case a unity which derives solely from the reality of Christ, that is to say from faith in this ultimate reality.

The conclusion is "that there is no real possibility of being a Christian outside the reality of the world and that there is no real worldly existence outside the reality of Jesus Christ" (p. 66).

Once again, we find a full continuity in Bonhoeffer's theology as he advances, spurred on by the personal experiences he had as a Christian and a churchman in the crises of the twentieth century, to find how the Christian faith must be lived *concretely,* here and now. The belief that God "is" for us in the community of the Church leads directly to the recognition that the Church as an institution cannot be walled around in order to contain the Living Christ there. Where the Church's faith was attacked by the forces of unfaith it was necessary to assert, "No salvation outside the Church!" But Bonhoeffer insisted that the Confessing Church was not then confessing against other church bodies in general—only "*in concretissimo* against the German Christian Church and against the neo-pagan divinization of the creature," where the will to destroy the Christian Church in Germany was at work (*No Rusty Swords,* pp. 337-338). A strategy of defense may be needful for us at a particular moment without our seeking thereby to limit God's work for His whole creation.

MAN AND THE WORLD

When Bonhoeffer speaks of "secular" life he usually is talking about our day-to-day involvement in the business of living—quite without any theory of the status of the secular. While his references to "religionless Christianity" have been interpreted as an invitation to throw out the concept of the supernatural and to concentrate our energies on improving the present lot of mankind, there is absolutely no indication that he ever wavered in his declared belief that wishing to build "the secular city" is the way of faithlessness.[41] Nor can his proposal for a "non-religious" interpretation of biblical concepts be read as a desire to find the "secular meaning" of the Gospel by accommodating the Word of God to the horizons of a contemporary world view.[42] Although reading in prison Carl-Friedrich von Weizsäcker's book *The World View of Physics* influenced him to take up a positive attitude to the "world come of age," it is quite mistaken to imagine that he regarded "secularization" as having decidedly Christian roots, on the model (say) of Gogarten's theories. His own "world view" when he was in prison is expressed in the confession, "Never have we realized, as we do to-day, how the world lies under the wrath and grace of God. . . . If we can save our souls unscathed from the débris of civilization, let us be satisfied with that" ("Thoughts on the Baptism of D. W. R.," *Letters,* May, 1944, pp. 183-184).

The "world come of age" is reckoned by Bonhoeffer to be a hopeful beginning for "clearing the decks for the God of the Bible" because it means "an abandonment of a false conception of God" (July 16, 1944, p. 220). "Religion" has encouraged, first, a metaphysical notion of God, and next, a God called in to meet our needs in the "inner life"—a "God of the gaps," since science takes care of the external world and its needs. But, in Bonhoeffer's eyes, God has never been a metaphysical postulate for faith, and the idea of "inwardness" he connects with the

---

[41]In the *Ethics* Bonhoeffer remarks (p. 87) how "Christian radicalism," in its world-improving quite as much as in its world-denying form, arises from "hatred of creation," and is an attempt to cast out devils through Beelzebub.

[42]"Meaning," says Bonhoeffer in the prison letters (August 21, 1944, p. 244) is only a translation of what the Bible means by "promise." This is in line with his continual insistence that reality is never encountered in abstract ideas but only in a concrete confrontation with the personal God.

Renaissance and not with the Bible. When Bonhoeffer speaks of a "worldly" interpretation of Christianity, he turns first of all to the Old Testament, a better understanding of which, he feels, helps us to rid ourselves of the view of Christianity as a religion of "salvation" in the style of pagan salvation-cults.[43] God's allowing Himself to be "edged out of the world" allows us to stop pretending that He is available as, when, and where we may wish to make use of Him.

Bonhoeffer, then, has no intention of trimming the historic Christian faith to encourage "secular" man to declare it "relevant."[44] That would be as mistaken as has been the former accommodation of the Gospel to fit the mould of "religious" man. The "world" he wishes to bring to the forefront of the Christian's attention is the sphere of earthly existence into which Christ, the Word made flesh, has come. It is the sphere of the *penultimate* deriving its meaning from the *ultimate* of faith. It is the sphere Barth's "positivism of revelation" has left to one side, uncared for. So we exhibit little confidence in the Gospel so long as we wait for people to feel helpless and afraid and ready to turn to the offer of religious consolation in some "last secret place." A better way would be "that we should not speak ill of man in his worldliness,

---

[43]"I am thinking over the problem at present how we may reinterpret in the manner 'of the world'—in the sense of the Old Testament and of John 1.14—the concepts of repentance, faith, justification, rebirth, sanctification and so on" (May 5, 1944, p. 169). Earlier in the same letter (p. 167) he writes: "What do I mean by 'interpret in a religious sense'? In my view, that means to speak on the one hand metaphysically, and on the other individualistically. Neither of these is relevant to the Bible message or to the man of to-day."

[44]"The *relevant* is not where the present age announces its claim before Christ, but where the present age stands before the claims of Christ" ("Interpretation of the New Testament," *No Rusty Swords*, p. 311).

but confront him with God at his strongest point. . ." (July 8, 1944, p. 214).

The mission for Christians in the modern world is one Bonhoeffer feels he understands. How it is to be achieved is another matter, and this occasions all the unanswered questions that fill the prison letters. Is there still room for the Church (as an organization)? How do we interpret biblical terms for men with no religious background? What *is* Christianity, and indeed who *is* Christ for us today? (The last question does not mean Bonhoeffer doubts Christ's relevance for today, but it reflects his uncertainty about where today the "boundaries" between the Church and the world, the two spheres of Christ's presence, are to be drawn.) One thing he is certain of. In an age that has almost forgotten the language of traditional faith, the Christian speaks more clearly in deeds than in words. So he writes of the Church: "She must not underestimate the importance of human example, which has its origin in the humanity of Jesus, and which is so important in the teaching of St. Paul. It is not abstract argument, but concrete example which gives her word emphasis and power" ("Outline for a Book," *Letters,* p. 240).

Another thing he thinks he is certain of. "We are proceeding towards a time of no religion at all: men as they are now simply cannot be religious any more" (April 30, 1944, p. 162). Here, speaking with the wisdom of hindsight, we can say that he was quite mistaken. He did not reckon with the staying power of *homo religiosus,* religious man who is always thinking he has outgrown his ancestral religion—and always either turning back to it or else seeking some substitute. Today, more than twenty years after Bonhoeffer's death, the traditional churches are, though shaken, yet not "changed beyond recognition," as he forecast. "Religion" is a prestige subject at our universities. And increasing around us are religious creeds of all kinds, including various brands of New Christianity (many of them claiming Bonhoeffer as their inspiration), each busily turning Christian faith into a salvation-cult by confidently explaining "how" Christ rescues us from other-worldliness into secularity, from transcendence into immanence, from the service of Yesterday's God into the service of the God of the Future.

Perhaps the major ambiguity present in Bonhoeffer's last phase of thought lies in his apparent implicit acceptance of a progressive view of history (a view he explicitly rejects) through his use of the term "man come of age."[45] Thus, while rightly condemning as futile an apologetic directed to calling back a past cultural situation, he seems to expect far too much from an apologetic directed to the present situation. On his own showing, changes in cultural patterns do not affect the continual evasion of the Word of God on the part of the *cor curvatum in se.*

If there is at present an opportunity, because of the decay of belief in a God who is merely a hypothesis, for a "clearing of the decks for the God of the Bible," there must be equally an empty house waiting for seven more dangerous man-made gods to take the place of the God-of-the-gaps-and-*deus-ex-machina* that has departed. There can be no possible correspondence between advance in human knowledge and maturity in Jesus Christ, so that present-day "religionless" man cannot be more open to an apologetic for faith than were his religious forefathers. Nor is this consideration chiefly one of an abstract analysis of the cultural world situation. It has important practical consequences for the life of the Church. If religionlessness is

---

[45]Kornelis H. Miskotte says in his *When the Gods Are Silent* (New York: Harper and Row, 1967, p. 81) that Bonhoeffer left the concept of the world come of age "somewhat undefined and that in any case he very much overestimated it."

not absolute, then the Gospel has to be preached to men who are not only estranged from Christian piety but also vulnerable to neo-pagan superstition, not only strongly world-affirming but also despairingly world-weary. The institutional Church is required in the world, not because the Gospel is a religious message but precisely because it is the only power that can turn men away from man-made religion. Without the visible Church, the proclamation that God's Kingdom has been brought into the world by Jesus Christ, and will come triumphantly when Christ comes again, will not be heard. Instead, men will fly to salvation-cults when they are fearful; or when they are confident they will deify their own schemes for raising Utopian Babel-towers, and sacrifice their brothers so that their will may be done on earth, even though the whole world must be laid waste in the process.

Bonhoeffer rightly condemned those who wish to be more "godly" than Christ, who did not scorn the human world, the manger in the stable and the cross of wood. He might also have gone on to doubt whether we can aspire to be more "religionless" than Christ, who, coming to supplant the teaching and the worship of synagogue and temple nevertheless Himself taught and worshipped in synagogue and temple. Bonhoeffer was not granted time— or the freedom of testing his ideas in the community of believers—to bring his theological work to full fruition. The sweep of his thinking that presses on to seek the significance of the whole Christ for the whole world has so much to teach us, that we do his memory little service by stopping short with his tentative explorations. But, without doubt, we cannot bypass the challenge that he presents to us to think through the static forms of our understanding of the Gospel to repossess its fullness for our own day. And the lesson of faithfulness is the lesson Bonhoeffer teaches. He, who so valued continuity in thought and in life, was not to be convinced that he had been a faithful steward of the Gospel of Jesus Christ in his generation unless he had continually kept before his eyes both the Eternal Christ and the changing face of the world to which Christ came, and for the sake of which He endured the cross. Bonhoeffer knew that the servant cannot be counted faithful who shrinks from going where his Lord has gone, or who, having been loved, withholds love from others.

4.   HIS VOICE IN OUR DAY

If the issues raised by Bonhoeffer's thinking during the prison period are ones he never fully clarified, this need not mean that we have to conclude, with Tillich, that "he didn't live long enough for us to know what he really thought."[46] Granted that he raised questions rather than supplied answers, and that some of the answers he gave raise more difficulties than they lay doubts to rest, it still remains true that the focus of his concern in those final months is plain enough. He asked what we must do in order to encounter Christ in our own generation and in the context of our cultural situation. And he believed he had come to have some insight into the problem, an insight producing such novel and startling phrases as "worldly holiness" and "religionless Christianity."

I have suggested already that his phrases have often been repeated glibly and squeezed into conceptual frames he himself would have most strongly repudiated. But the point is that, if we have heard Bonhoeffer at all, we have heard him calling us to take up the task he laid down. It is not enough simply to note the things he said, and voice our assent or dissent. He demands of us that we hear his voice speaking to us in our day of the concerns he felt in his. There is even a sense in which misunderstanding his

---

[46]See above, p. 21.

message is understanding it, when it leads us to share his conviction that the Church must get out of its rut and meet the challenge of the present age. Yet, misunderstanding can be disastrous if we imagine we can easily see that which was no more than dimly visible to him, or if we use his words in order to accept proposals that for him were ruled out from the start.

So it is necessary to look in considerably greater detail at a few of the issues discussed in the last chapter, where the controversial themes of the *Letters and Papers from Prison* rose up to claim our attention. By making the focus of our inquiry the nature of Christian discipleship, the inner cohesion of Bonhoeffer's thinking may reveal itself.

THE "WORLDLY" CHRISTIAN

One passage in the prison letters (July 21, 1944, pp. 225-226) is particularly illuminating, because it takes off from the position Bonhoeffer held when he wrote *The Cost of Discipleship,* where the emphasis was upon opposition to the world. Even then, he remarks (p. 226), he felt sure that the Christian should not desire consciously to become a saint, but rather should seek the gift of faith. He continues (p. 226),

> Later I discovered and am still discovering up to this very moment that it is only by living completely in this world that one learns to believe. One must abandon every attempt to make something of oneself, whether it be a saint, a converted sinner, a churchman (the priestly type, so-called!), a righteous man or an unrighteous one, a sick man or a healthy one. This is what I mean by worldliness— taking life in one's stride, with all its duties and problems, its successes and failures, its experiences and helplessness. It is in such a life that we throw ourselves utterly in the arms of God and participate in his sufferings in the world [taking seriously, not our own sufferings but those of God

in the world] and watch with Christ in Gethsemane. That is faith, that is *metanoia,* and that is what makes a man and a Christian (cf. Jeremiah 45). How can success make us arrogant or failure lead us astray, when we participate in the sufferings of God by living in this world? [. . . when we share in God's sufferings through a life of this kind?]

This is what I mean by worldliness—taking life in one's stride. Bonhoeffer has already explained (pp. 225-226),

I don't mean the shallow this-worldliness of the enlightened, of the busy, the comfortable or the lascivious. It's something much more profound than that, something [characterized by discipline] in which the knowledge of death and resurrection is ever present.

Unlike some of the advocates of a "secular" Christianity who have claimed to follow his lead, he never forgets that the arena of human activity in which we live our everyday lives is no more than the "penultimate" that gains its meaning from the "ultimate." The reference to death and resurrection here, too, cannot refer to the fact that all life can be viewed as containing within itself death-and-resurrection experiences that give human existence a "depth dimension." The reference is to the death and resurrection of Christ; and we should remember that Bonhoeffer categorically refuses to demythologize the resurrection.

Taking life in one's stride and living unreservedly in all that it brings, then, is accepting the world God has given to us as the place of our pilgrimage. It is not accepting the world as the only world we know. Our horizons extend beyond earthly existence, since the ultimate has been revealed to us beyond the penultimate. The life of the Christian embraces in faith the evidence of things not seen, evidence enabling him to journey through things seen with a confidence the unbelieving "world" cannot know. The temper of this-worldliness assumes, either that life will yield what we hope for "with a little bit of luck," or else that life is essentially meaningless and is given value only when we admit this and damn the consequences. (The latter interpretation is usually dignified by being called "choosing authentic existence.") Bonhoeffer, however, speaks of throwing ourselves without reserve in the arms of God; and his language here is strongly reminiscent of St. Paul's words about having learned both to be abased and to abound, sufficient in all things through the One who strengthens him (Phil. 4:11-13). Such an attitude is possible only to the man who knows himself to be a traveller bound for another country, and therefore prepared to travel light. As Bonhoeffer wrote in a different connection,[47] "How can men endure earthly tensions if they know nothing of the tension between earth and heaven?"

It is surely significant that Bonhoeffer turned to speak with so easy a grace about taking life in one's stride at the very time when he had just heard of the failure of the plot to assassinate Hitler, and knew how fateful this event must prove for himself and for many of those who stood nearest to him in blood and affection. He must have read often and pondered the scriptural passage (Col. 3:1-4):

> If then you have been raised with Christ, seek the things that are above, where Christ is, seated at the right hand of God. Set your minds on things that are above, not on things that are on earth. For you have died, and your life is hid with Christ in God. When Christ who is our life appears, then you also will appear with him in glory.

Only by living in the spirit of this passage could he have endured the fear-clouded tedium of imprisonment and finally walked to his execution saying that for him it was

---

[47]See above, p. 47.

the beginning of life. Yet this is the man who wrote in the *Ethics* about the mistake of "thinking in terms of two spheres," and who, faced with the knowledge that he could not hope ever to be a free man again, said he was discovering that the believer must live "completely in this world."

There is no real contradiction, so long as it is remembered that Bonhoeffer's continual effort was to read the Bible in such a way that it could address contemporary men. He would not be bound in his reading by a "religious" tradition, however venerable. But neither would he allow the prejudices of contemporary culture to dictate what the Bible could, or could not, say to man at large. The separation which he deplored between the two spheres of the sacred and the secular was, as he saw it, a cultural effect which had given rise to the individualistic other-worldliness of pietism. (And, incidentally, he attributed this effect to a movement first visible in the "secular" rather than in the "religious" sphere.[48]) Thus, to live completely in this world was for him no denial of the scriptural understanding of this world as a passing world never to be loved for itself; it was an affirmation of the scriptural understanding of this world as God's creation, spoiled by sin and groaning until it finds redemption, yet never abandoned by its Creator, and encompassed by the condescending love that shone radiantly within its darkness in the face of Jesus Christ, the Incarnate Word, the Light of the world.

---

[48]See the prison letter of July 8, 1944 (p. 214): "The discovery of inwardness, so-called, derives from the Renaissance, from Petrarch perhaps. The 'heart' in the biblical sense is not the inward life, but the whole man in relation to God. The view that man lives just as much from outwards to inwards as from inwards to outwards is poles apart from the view that his essential nature is to be understood from his intimate background."

Bonhoeffer began his theological work by insisting that Christ must really *be* in this world—and not exist merely as an idea in our minds or as "non-objective" reality we discover by contemplating the depths of our consciousness. Christ was actually among us, Emmanuel (God-with-us), the Incarnate One. He still remains in the world He did not despise to enter as the Humiliated One. He lives through the Holy Spirit active in the Church. This theme continued in Bonhoeffer's thought and finds eloquent expression in the *Ethics* (p. 70):

> The dark and evil world must not be abandoned to the devil. It must be claimed for Him who has won it by His incarnation, His death and His resurrection. Christ gives up nothing of what He has won. . . . That God loved the world and reconciled it with Himself in Christ is the central message proclaimed in the New Testament. . . . The acceptance of the world by God is a miracle of the divine compassion.

There is indeed a love for the world that is enmity toward God (Jas. 4:4), says Bonhoeffer, because it is love of the world *as the world understands itself*. But it is the task of the Church to proclaim to the world the reconciliation to which it is blind.

The theme of Christian "worldliness" takes up the same theme from the point of view of the Christian disciple, who, though not "of" the world, is nevertheless called to be "in" it (John 17:13-19). Our Christian witness cannot be a disembodied thing. And, equally, our Christian concern cannot be restricted to the limits we may wish to draw around it. The temptation of Christian pietism is to pine after a timeless spiritual world, and to withdraw into a congenial company of like-minded people hoping to save individuals "out of" the world. The result is the religious view of life. The religious man keeps a corner of his existence—greater or smaller as the case may be—for

God. He thinks of his religion as something he turns to within the church sanctuary, the moments he spares for private devotions; or as something he expresses in pious phrases thrown into ordinary conversation, and in such "witness" as he may perhaps give to his beliefs when talk among friends takes a "serious" turn. If he is not (as he would express it himself) particularly religious, then he does not think about God at all except when, in a "boundary situation" of being in deep distress or in fear of death, his normal matter-of-fact relationship to the world around him is disrupted. But God demands the whole of life, and not just the religious edges of it.[49]

If religion were the answer to the question of life's purpose and meaning, then our troubles would be caused by too little religion. More religion would put things right. However, the Christian Gospel is hardly to be understood as primarily a call to be very religious. As Bonhoeffer sees it, the Gospel is first of all a recall to the truth about the world under God to which the Bible directed us. The truth we need to know is that God first made us created beings so that we might remember our Creator continually all our days; and that He has saved us, in spite of ourselves and in the face of our sinful rebellion against His laws, in Jesus Christ. Thus the Christian who responds to the divine forgiveness cannot turn to serve his Saviour anywhere else except in that place where God has set him—and that place is the world. His role is to be conformed to the image of God's Son, who did not please Himself, but accepted in humility the sphere of human flesh, that He might be the first-born among many brethren (Rom. 8:29).

---

[49]Cf. the prison letter, July 18, 1944 (p. 224): "The religious act is always something partial, faith is always something whole, an act involving the whole life. Jesus does not call men to a new religion, but to life."

THE SECRET DISCIPLINE OF A CHRISTIAN

When Bonhoeffer began to consider seriously the possibility of a religionless Christianity, he naturally was confronted very soon with the problem of how a "religionless" Christian was to stand in connection with worship and all the traditional external aids to the Christian life that had been known in the Church as *the means of grace.* Indeed, the very existence of the Church as a "religious" institution was called in question. He writes about this at length in the prison letter of April 30, 1944 (pp. 161-166), though almost entirely in the form of questions to which no definite answers are suggested. The main section of the letter concentrating on the topic ends with the following passage (p. 164):

> In what way are we in a religionless and secular sense Christians, in what way are we the *Ekklesia,* "those who are called forth," not conceiving of ourselves religiously as specially favoured, but as wholly belonging to the world? Then Christ is no longer an object of religion, but something quite different, indeed and in truth the Lord of the world. Yet what does that signify? What is the place of worship and prayer in an entire absence of religion? Does the secret discipline, or, as the case may be, the distinction (which you have met with me before) between penultimate and ultimate, at this point acquire fresh importance?

Here the linking of "the secret discipline" (*Arkandisziplin*) to the distinction between the ultimate and the penultimate is perhaps the key to the direction of Bonhoeffer's thinking. The latter terms have been chosen by him to replace the terminology referring to "this world" and "the next world," largely because he thinks they may help us to avoid the danger of imagining we have to choose absolutely between them. As we have seen, Bonhoeffer recognizes that there is an absolute contradiction between "this world" (in the sense of the world lying under the power of sin) and the Kingdom announced by Jesus Christ, a Kingdom that is "not of this world." Nevertheless, the way of thinking that leaves the created order to the devil and strives solely to direct our minds to preparing ourselves for "another" world is one that forgets how God acted in the Incarnate Son, "through him to reconcile to himself all things, whether on earth or in heaven, making peace by the blood of the cross" (Col. 1:20). The Christian who writes off the world as lost cannot pray in the words of his Master that God's will may be done on earth as in heaven. The distinction between the ultimate and the penultimate, on the other hand, reminds us that earth stands under heaven. In itself it is nothing. Yet, as the object of God's redeeming love, it is infinitely precious and lays upon us obligations that bind us until our earthly life ends.

The Christian, then, is to live as (penultimately) wholly belonging to the world. His life is to witness to the fact that Christ is the Lord of the world. He is not a Christian because he makes a religious profession but because he is committed to participating in his Lord's suffering on behalf of the world, trusting himself to God's providential care.[50] What has this to do with "the secret discipline"? For light on Bonhoeffer's phrase we can refer to

---

[50]That trust in Providence is a fair paraphrase of "throwing ourselves utterly in the arms of God" seems to be confirmed by Bonhoeffer's references to Providence in the prison letters. He writes (April 22, 1944, p. 159), "It never occurs to me how different everything would be to-day if only I had acted differently in the past. I can't help feeling that everything has taken its natural course; it has all been inevitable, straightforward, directed by a higher providence." Earlier (February 21, 1944, p. 138) he speaks of the necessity to defy "fate" at some times and to submit to it at others—and thereby to discover the guidance of providence. "Faith demands this elasticity of behaviour." Here is another aspect of taking life in one's stride—under the control of grace!

The Cost of Discipleship, where a section in Part Two is headed "Of the Hidden Character of the Christian Life." This section is a commentary on the text "Take heed that ye do not your righteousness before men, to be seen of them" (Matt. 6:1). Its central theme is summed up in the following comment on prayer (p. 146):

> Prayer is the supreme instance of the hidden character of the Christian life. It is the antithesis of self-display. When men pray they have ceased to know themselves, and know only God whom they call upon. Prayer does not aim at any direct effect on the world; it is addressed to God alone, and is therefore the perfect example of undemonstrative action.

Prayer does not have to be always private to be secret, notes Bonhoeffer. Its hidden character consists of the fact that it does not try to be a good work to justify the one who prays (or the company of believers) but is a response of faith to the Father who sees in secret.

It would seem that the hiddenness of the *Arkandiszi-plin* is not primarily that it is something kept from the gaze of the unbelieving world and practiced unostentatiously by Christians, either alone or in fellowship, but that it is a direct link between the believer or the worshipping community and God. It is the means whereby men living on earth have access to heaven, bringing the penultimate into living contact with the ultimate. In *The Cost of Discipleship* Bonhoeffer insists (p. 142) that the hidden righteousness is essentially hidden from *ourselves,* in that it is not won by our claiming it for ourselves but by placing our faith in God and allowing Him to produce in us effects of which we remain unconscious. Only thus can the Christian life be natural and free from sanctimoniousness and pharisaic pride.

The secret discipline to be followed in the Christian life, therefore, is an expression in the sphere of worship of the distinction between the ultimate and the penultimate. The Christian lives in the penultimate, yet always with the knowledge that the penultimate derives its meaning and purpose from the ultimate. The Christian lives also the life of human values found in the service of others, yet always deriving his power to love his fellows unsentimentally from the divine grace he discovers through the secret discipline. He does not say to the non-Christian, "You want to be a good man. I am able to live a truly human life because I worship God. You will never be fully human until you, too, find the need for worship." To make such a claim (even silently) would be to shift the basis of trust from God to religion. Instead, the Christian worships because this discipline goes with the response of faith, and faith will not be kept alive without it. Worship follows the action of divine grace within the individual, who can say with the Psalmist (Psalm 51:6), "Behold, thou desirest truth in the inward being; therefore teach me wisdom in my secret heart." But worship cannot be made into a law for the unbeliever, the person who has not yet learned that truth is from God.

Bonhoeffer also seems to have thought that the secret discipline would, in fact, be literally a hidden affair for some time to come. This belief of his came from his conviction that the Church had been for so long trading on its religious prestige that it had largely ceased to be the means through which the Word spoke with power. In his "Thoughts on the Baptism of D.W.R." (*Letters,* May 21, 1944, p. 187) he writes of how the infant to be baptized will have the liturgy of baptism said over him, all unknowing. But, he adds, we too are being driven back to first principles. The great words of the Christian proclamation have become for us problematic and remote. He continues:

In the traditional rite and ceremonies we are groping after something new and revolutionary without being able to understand it or utter it yet. That is our own fault. During these years the Church has fought for self-preservation as though it were an end in itself, and has thereby lost its chance to speak a word of reconciliation to mankind and the world at large. So our traditional language must perforce become powerless and remain silent, and our Christianity to-day will be confined to praying for and doing right by our fellow men. Christian thinking, speaking and organization must be reborn out of this praying and this action.

A similar though more enigmatic statement appears earlier (May 5, 1944) when Bonhoeffer is criticizing Karl Barth's "positivism of revelation." What is wrong with Barth's position, Bonhoeffer thinks, is that it prescribes the entire structure of traditional theology as the needful diet of the Church, in such a way that everything in it has to be accepted in a lump—swallowed as a whole or not at all. He objects (pp. 168-169):

That is not in accordance with the Bible. There are degrees of perception and degrees of significance, i.e. a secret discipline must be re-established whereby the *mysteries* of the Christian faith are preserved from profanation. The positivist doctrine of revelation makes it too easy for itself, setting up, as in the ultimate analysis it does, a law of faith, and mutilating what is, by the incarnation of Christ, a gift for us. The place of religion is taken by the Church—that is, in itself, as the Bible teaches it should be—but the world [in some degree] is made to depend upon itself and left to its own devices, and that is all wrong.

Here the references to degrees of perception and significance, and to positivism of revelation setting up a law of faith, have a decided connection with his remarks, in connection with the baptism, about the Church having been too concerned over its own preservation. Bonhoeffer, apparently, is convinced that when the Church makes submission to doctrinal statements the badge of belonging to the Christian community, it sins against the hiddenness of the character of the Christian life.[51] Trying to put everything on one level, it misses the biblical warning that the letter can kill and only the spirit make alive. Faith cannot be a law, cannot be laid down by an external standard; and therefore the roots of faith must be nourished by the *mysteries* that are made known to us in worship, since there God plants in our secret heart a wisdom that eludes doctrinal definition. A Church that has said too much, too easily, about the life of faith should on that account realize that its duty may be to keep silent until its actual life catches up with its loudly declared professions.[52] Then it will know how to speak, and will speak with power, for it will have proved that it really cares for the world it dares to challenge in the name of Christ, who gave His life for all mankind.

GOD'S GUIDING HAND IN A WORLD COME OF AGE

The last of the prison letters opens with these words (August 23, 1944, p. 245):

[51]Cf. *Letters,* August 3, 1944, the "Outline for a Book," chapter 2 (e), "What do we really believe? I mean believe in such a way as to stake our whole lives upon it? The problem of the Apostles' Creed? 'What must I believe?' the wrong question . . . . Barth and the Confessing Church have encouraged us to entrench ourselves behind the 'faith of the Church,' and evade the honest question, what is our real and personal belief?" (pp. 238-239).

[52]Cf. Regin Prenter, "Only when one interprets secret discipline as an act of repentance on the part of the church, which was there for herself instead of for the world, is it possible to make sense of Bonhoeffer's apparently contradictory attitude to Karl Barth's orthodoxy" ("Bonhoeffer and Karl Barth's Positivism of Revelation" in *World Come of Age,* ed. R. G. Smith, p. 104). Prenter recognizes the importance of the concept of *Arkandisziplin* in Bonhoeffer, deploring the way in which it has been overlooked. His whole discussion of the concept is most stimulating, and I am much indebted to it.

> Please don't ever get anxious or worried about me, but don't forget to pray for me—I'm sure you don't! I am so sure of God's guiding hand, and I hope I shall never lose that certainty.

This completely unselfconscious use of the language of traditional piety is as typical of Bonhoeffer as is his boldness in thrusting aside accepted opinions and conventional valuations. In the same letter (July 21, 1944) quoted at the beginning of the present chapter, where he enlarges on his understanding of Christian worldliness, he speaks about there being a time for laying aside theological discussion. He writes (p. 225):

> It's true these theological problems are always occupying my mind, but there are times when I am just content to live the life of faith without worrying about its problems. In such moods I take a simple pleasure in the text of the day, and yesterday's and to-day's were particularly good (July 20th: Psalm 20.8: Romans 8.31; 21.7: Psalm 23.1: John 10.24). Then I go back to Paul Gerhardt's wonderful hymns, which never pall.

The simple believer, the sophisticated student of culture, and the acute theologian were, however, one man. Bonhoeffer's integrity—which is part of the reason for his extraordinary appeal to all kinds of persons—makes it impossible for us to imagine that he simply adopted different *personae* at will without allowing these to be critically aware of one another.

Remembering this, we can be certain that one of the sources of his conception of the "world come of age" was his trust in the guiding hand of God. If men today were finding religion less and less a feature of their daily lives, this could only be because this development was part of God's intention for His world. If, as he wrote in the letter of June 8, 1944 (p. 195), "what we call 'God' is being more and more edged out of life, losing more and more ground," this is no cause for churchmen to despair. It is only nervous souls who will ask what is to become of God and of the Church when religion fails. For the one thing we can be certain about is that God remains ever Lord of the earth and the Preserver of His Church. Instead of thinking that this wicked world must somehow have turned very much more wicked, we should ask ourselves whether what we call "God" is not exactly what God is asking us to leave behind.

Bonhoeffer's concept of the secret discipline is closely connected with his entire willingness to believe that the development undermining the authority of "the Christian religion" as a cultural force is a consequence of divine Providence. We must remember that the secret discipline is, in the first place, something hidden from *ourselves*. That is, our prayers have no values simply because we make the decision—guided, no doubt, by the force of our religious education—to pray. Only God can bless our prayers by giving us the Holy Spirit to pray on our behalf (Rom. 8:26). Similarly, our beliefs have no value as mental constructs (hypotheses) apart from God's gift of faith enabling us to know the only true God, and Jesus Christ whom He has sent (John 17:3). So the attitude that confronts the world and says that it is imperative to believe certain things, or to pray in certain forms, is one that inevitably leads to profaning the Christian myster-ies. Just as the Jews in the time of Jeremiah insisted that faith was bound to the temple, and just as the Judaizers of St. Paul's time insisted that faith was bound to circumcision, equally the modern upholders of the ideal of a cultural Christendom insist that faith is bound to a picture of the universe organized around a concept called "God." All three attempt vainly to set up a law that shall guarantee faith; and the result is a religious husk out of which the kernel of faith has fallen.

Note that Bonhoeffer does not deny that the world can be understood rightly only when we see it continually upheld by its Creator, and that this is how the man of faith sees it. What he denies is that accepting the hypothesis that the world finds its completion in a transcendent entity called "God" is a step in the direction of faith in the Living God. Therefore, why demand that the man who lives "without God in the world" (Gal. 2:12) must take this step as a condition of being confronted with the claims of the Gospel of Jesus Christ? For Bonhoeffer, the apologetic device of using natural theology as a preparation for the Gospel is valueless, whether we are dealing with those who are prepared to consider the theistic hypothesis or with those who reject it out of hand. The world has come of age in this respect: that it has found the theistic hypothesis to be of no practical utility. Bonhoeffer opines that it is pointless, ignoble, and un-Christian to treat modern men as though they could still be forced into admitting that they need the theistic hypothesis for living. We should realize that it is a waste of time to plead with our contemporaries to admit that the temper of present-day culture is other than it shows itself to be. When education was in the hands of churchmen, laymen accepted meekly enough the proposition that the final explanation of the universe was a religious one. Today, abstract arguments about a Prime Mover have no obvious utility for the offspring of a technologically oriented culture who think in terms of manipulating the environment in the interests of human well-being. To say that the modern man's understanding of the universe is shallow and metaphysically deficient may be correct, yet beside the point. He has also learned a great deal about the nature of the world he lives in, and how to control it to solve the practical problems of living in it. And he knows that, in this particular area of knowl-

edge, metaphysics and religion have not been particularly
helpful.

Why Bonhoeffer objected to the metaphysical God was
that he believed this "God" existed (from our point of
view) to answer questions we posed about the nature of
the universe. To this extent this deity was a "stop-gap"
God, a hypothesis proposed to answer our questions. But
the Living God is not a question-answerer. He is an ever
present help—and also the disturber of our complacency.
This is why Bonhoeffer speaks so often about God belonging in the center of life: "the Beyond in our midst." So he
writes in the letter of May 25, 1944 (pp. 190-191):

> We should find God in what we do know, not in what we
> don't; not in outstanding problems, but in those we have
> already solved. . . . It just isn't true to say that Christianity
> alone has the answers. In fact the Christian answers are no
> more conclusive or compelling than any of the others. . . .
> Christ is the centre of life, and in no sense did he come to
> answer our unsolved problems. . . . In Christ there are no
> Christian problems.

Once again, we should note, Bonhoeffer is not saying that
the Christian understanding of life is not conclusive for
the believer. He is saying that there is no apologetic value
in asking the unbeliever to embrace Christianity because
it explains the universe more completely than rival philos-
ophies of life. The Christian, indeed, must often admit
that he does not know the explanation of why the world
is as it is. He will probably say that he simply accepts
many things as mysteries in relation to which he accepts
in faith what he cannot understand. But he does know
Him whom he has believed (II Tim. 1:12). And so, in this
spirit, Bonhoeffer felt that he could put problems behind
him—even theological problems that needed to be grap-
pled with—and take simple pleasure in the text for the

day, holding to the certainty of God's guiding hand upon his daily life.

It is against this background that we should interpret his words about the world come of age. He never subscribed to the idea of a progressive development (an idea he attributed to idealistic philosophy), and certainly not in the realm of theology. Farthest from his mind would be any claim for our age to have outgrown, through its superior sophistication, a naive idea of God "up there" and thus to have reached the stage where it was ready to push on to a better idea of God in the depths of our being, or in the creative purpose of the historical process as such, or in the human will to community. Not for him, ever, the demythologizing approach! Instead, he writes (July 18, 1944, p. 224):

> When we speak of God in a non-religious way, we must not gloss over the ungodliness of the world, but expose it in a new light. Now that it has come of age, the world is more godless, and perhaps for that very reason nearer to God than ever before.

To speak of God in a non-religious way is very different, it would seem, from attempting to show "the secular meaning of the gospel"—in the sense of producing a God-hypothesis acceptable to a world that has ceased to give credence to the God of the Bible. No, the world is always godless, apart from God's grace gifted to it. The world come of age is not a world progressed to the perfect theological insight that non-worship during a time of the absence of God is actually the appropriate way of being a Christian in the twentieth century. If the world is possibly nearer to God than ever before, it is precisely on account of its having no truck with theology, either traditional or modish, as it goes on its godless way. Its sole advantage is that it is in the position of the blasphemer whose curses (according to Luther's saying, cherished by

Bonhoeffer) are more acceptable to God than all the hallelujahs of the pious. The godless man, fighting against God or spurning Him, may meet Him face to face more quickly than the person who calls himself a converted sinner but walks through life in the strength of his own self-approving conscience rather than forgetting himself under God's guiding hand.

MAY GOD LEAD US TO HIMSELF!

After speaking of the worldly holiness that takes life in its stride (July 21, 1944), Bonhoeffer adds a personal note (p. 227):

> I think you get my meaning, though I put it so briefly. I am glad I have been able to learn it, and I know I could only have done so along the road I have travelled. So I am grateful and content with the past and the present. Perhaps you are surprised at the personal tone of this letter, but if for once I want to talk like this, to whom else should I say it? May God in his mercy lead us through these times. But above all may he lead us to himself!

Nowhere else, perhaps, does Bonhoeffer declare more directly the heart of his message and the place where he stands. In this confession we are allowed to see his vision of the commitment to Christian discipleship, with its openness to all that life may bring, and its conviction that answers to our questions are to be found alone in the concrete duties we are called on to perform along the pilgrim way.

As a Christian disciple Bonhoeffer asks God to lead him and his contemporaries through the world of his time—to the end that he and they may rest in the divine love that has made us all, preserves us, and goes before us to prepare a place for us. That in itself ought to be enough to let us know that religionless Christianity cannot be made into a shibboleth to test the appropriateness of the

Gospel for present-day man, a law of faith to which every expression of modern Christianity must be made to conform. Bonhoeffer discovered the need for emphasizing the worldly dimension of the Christian life by following the road along which God had led him. And it does not follow that we, who walk our road a quarter of a century after his death, will find the identical emphasis to be required in our day; or that we will have nothing to add and nothing to subtract with reference to his findings. We too have to ask, as he did, what Christianity really is, and indeed who Christ really is, for us today. Our day is unlike his day, not simply because it is a later day, but because it is a day when a whole host of theories concerning religionless and secular and God-less varieties of Christianity have been widely publicized. In spite of his criticism of Karl Barth's positivism of revelation, Bonhoeffer considered himself one of the "modern" theologians who stood with Barth as the latter "called the God of Jesus Christ into the lists against religion" (June 8, 1944, p. 198). Now that Barth is no longer "modern" but widely considered "old hat," who is the God that is being called into the lists today?

Following Barth, Bonhoeffer reacted against the liberalism dominant in the earlier years of the century; and in the prison letters he described liberalism's mistake as being "that it allowed the world the right to assign Christ his place in that world" (June 8, 1944, p. 197). It would seem that the same mistake is now being made in the name of Bonhoeffer and under the label of his phrase "the nonreligious (secular) interpretation of biblical concepts." For, if biblical terminology is abandoned in favor of so-called equivalent concepts relating to man's ethical and social experience, then the Christian Gospel is not related to worldly experience, it is reduced to it. And, where no place is allowed for the "secret discipline," then

Christ is assigned His place in the world as a captive forbidden to speak for Himself. In such a procedure the godlessness of the world is not exposed in the slightest degree. On the contrary, the world's estimate of what it has the right to demand of man is made the measure of the Christian's duty. In place of the freedom of faith, the individual is set under a law of good works demanded by the secular order.

This state of affairs is at least partly the result of the fact that Bonhoeffer never developed any "exposure" of the godlessness of the world.[53] There was no urgent call for him to do so, of course, when the whole weight of his thinking was on the side of discovering a Christian obliga-

---

[53]Cf. Reginald H. Fuller (the translator of *Letters and Papers*): "Of course, there must be a critique of the autonomous world from the perspective of the God of the Bible. Bonhoeffer offers little or nothing here. Therein lies his chief limitation, and the cause of so much misunderstanding—as though Bonhoeffer accepted the world come of age at its own self-evaluation. In rebelling against the God of religion it did not as a consequence accept the God of the Bible. But Bonhoeffer never clearly says so. He never tries to get under the world's skin, to show that everything is not well with it after all in spite of its having come of age, i.e., its legitimate securing of autonomy over against the false God of religion" ("World Come of Age: A Second Look at Bonhoeffer," in *Conflicting Images of Man*, ed. William Nicholls, p. 161).

Fuller points out how easily we might assume that Bonhoeffer's understanding of "the world come of age" must be identical with the understanding of those thinkers of the Enlightenment (prominently Kant and Hegel) who introduced the phrase—although Bonhoeffer never accepted the viewpoint of the Enlightenment. He thinks that it was fear of "methodism" that prevented Bonhoeffer from attempting any critique of the newly matured world's self-estimate. Yet the mere lack of time and opportunity is reason enough for Bonhoeffer's silence here. He never said half what he hoped to say about disentangling Christianity from religion. Why should he turn to what was, then, a less urgent task? Besides, in his earlier works he had made clear how the world is ever corrupted by sin as well as kept from total destruction by grace.

tion not "to leave the world to its own devices." But now the boot is on the other foot. With the Church inviting the world, as the current phrase has it, "to write the agenda," the pressing need is to see that the world is not competent, from the Christian viewpoint, to assign to the Church the tasks it wishes it to perform on its behalf. The Christian is indeed the servant of his brethren, and slave of all for Christ's sake. He is not, however, slave of the world for the world's sake. He may render to Caesar the things that are Caesar's—and must do so as a citizen of earth; but he is also a citizen of a Kingdom that is not of this world. His service is, finally, God's to command. And neither city-planner, nor sociologist, nor historian of culture, nor any of the pundits guarding the repositories of human wisdom can instruct him authoritatively on how to live the Christian life among his neighbors, though he should be ready to listen attentively to them all. We need not doubt that God is speaking to us through the secular agencies in society, guiding us through these our times. Yet it is not through them that we become certain of His guidance, and it is not their mediation that leads us to Him.

Bonhoeffer speaks more than once of life being a polyphony, a multi-dimensional affair. Taking life in one's stride means being able to move freely, not tied to one dimension. Yet the unity of life is guaranteed, ultimately, by faith. It is faith that provides the *cantus firmus* making possible a full and perfect sound in life's music. Following this line of thinking, we are led to wonder whether Bonhoeffer fully considered how the polyphony of life was to be maintained in the entire absence of religion. Religion, it is true, belongs to fallen human existence. There will be no religion in heaven. There is no temple in the New Jerusalem (Rev. 21:22)! But perhaps Barth is more realistic at this point than Bonhoeffer when he says that the religious Christian is parallel to the justified sinner. God uses religion, too, in His merciful work for our salvation, since for us human beings there is no way in which faith is reflected in our consciousness except religiously.

When Bonhoeffer lays aside his problems and turns to take rest in the promises of God, he takes a simple—and very human—pleasure in the texts for the day. He could not do so unless these were mediated to him through the religious tradition in which he was reared. The theology that occupies his mind as he wrestles with the need for keeping wholeness in our engagement with the world as we seek to be conformed to the pattern of Christ: this also is the product of a long religious tradition that he lays hold upon. Even in his reaction against religion he is religiously motivated, remaining very much a spiritual son of Luther and of the long line of religious thinkers of the Western Church.

For Bonhoeffer the religious atmosphere he moves in is, for the most part, taken as much for granted as the air he breathes. To change the metaphor, it is a windowpane he never notices except when he sees how dirty it has become. We, however, in our present situation may be aware also that the glass, which is frequently so smeared that it prevents us from looking through it to discern God's wide skies, has, nevertheless, a positive function. Without it the human house would be so dark we might never learn to use our eyes at all.

It is to the highest degree interesting that, whenever he says in the prison letters he is going to give a sample of the non-religious interpretation of biblical concepts, Bonhoeffer never actually does so. Instead, he veers away on the track of a historical analysis of the growth of secularism. Or he simply writes that it is too hard to be attempted at present. Could it be that he had set himself a problem he knew within himself to be impossible? Certainly, when he forgets his problem he takes up gladly and spontaneously the human way to God, the religious way. Gerhardt's hymns, the familiar liturgy, the festivals of the Church, Luther's habit of making the sign of the cross at prayer, as well as the verses of the Bible that stand as remembered milestones along the road of the years marked by its devotional use since childhood: all these provide the basis for the secret discipline. And the secret discipline itself is at bottom no more than a particular use of the religious exercises that have shaped down the ages "the Christian religion."

Bonhoeffer has left us an incomplete picture, through his concentration upon the alienation of the "newly matured" world from its religious past, both of the present situation of the Christian believer and of the horizons of the unbelieving man in our times. For example, he wrote (June 8, 1944, pp. 197-198) that Tillich's effort to interpret the evolution of the world in a religious sense had failed, since the world "felt entirely *mis*understood, and rejected the imputation." Since that time, however, Tillich has gained a much more respectful hearing from the world at large. In the same letter Bonhoeffer dismissed (p. 196) "the secularized off-shoots of Christian theology, the existentialist philosophers and the psychotherapists" as persons who would never influence any but "a small number of intellectuals, of degenerates" and the like with their doctrine that man-come-of-age was not happy and contented. The dismissal was surely premature.

It seems that Bonhoeffer's forecast was far too optimistic and over-simple. He hoped that the waning of the influence of the religious traditions of Christendom would be a clearing of the decks for the God of the Bible. What we have seen is a varied flow of religious or quasi-religious reactions throwing up to the surface a medley of competing analyses of the "predicament" of contemporary man, who is asked one moment to affirm himself in a meaningless universe, and the next to celebrate the death of God as an event restoring hope to the human enterprise. Meanwhile, metaphysical gods are being proposed on all sides by religious thinkers, who assure us that a metaphysic of *becoming* will overcome the deficiencies of a metaphysic of *being,* or that *panentheism* will be the God-hypothesis to succeed *theism.* Secular world views are set up in the place of religious world views, and commended to the Christian—as though a religion were any less a religion by sticking on itself the label "non-religious." (This particular ploy has been a favorite one for a long time with militant minority denominations, who virtuously describe themselves as "not a denomination.")

Bonhoeffer left the door open to such travesties of his "non-religious" interpretation of the Gospel because he looked back along the road he had travelled and took for granted that the only deity a Christian could confess in this religiously uninterested age must be the God of the Bible. He did not expose the ungodliness of the world in such a way as to uncover its unshakable faith in religion, its determination to have gods to bow down before of its own choosing—even if such gods had to be named "the absence of the presence of God" or "the God who *shall be,* the God who succeeds the God who *was* and *is not.*"

But Bonhoeffer has still so much to teach us, because he fixed his faith, beyond all religion, on the God who has revealed Himself. The record of the God of the Bible in His dealings with men is for Bonhoeffer one that cannot be demythologized. It is not something we can interpret out of our native stock of religious ideas. Myths of salvation have sprung in plenty from humanity's religious imagination. But the God of Abraham and Father of our Lord Jesus Christ has redeemed us, in a manner beyond all our powers of imagining, and set us the joyful task of finding Him continually in the center of our lives. The Christ who lived in the world is the Eternal Christ who calls us to live in the world and know the power that is made perfect in weakness (II Cor. 12:9).

As we learn from Bonhoeffer how worldly the Christian life should be, we can learn also from his example (though not, directly, from his precept) how necessary is the religious dimension of human existence. If God is to lead us to Himself, the path will be one prepared by religious institutions, religious observances, and religious habits of mind and conscience. It was upon this that Bonhoeffer depended for the content of his secret discipline. But he knew that the existence of the path will not in itself lead us toward God. There is no means of preventing us from using it to walk in the very opposite direction, taking the way of self-will; the "fleshly" way that does not discern the Spirit but leads us away from the liberty of Christ into the bondage of religious law; and the idolatrous way that wishes to construct its own truth in place of the true Word revealed to us by God Himself. Religion can never be the end, though it may be the means—provided we never confuse means and end. There is one end to which the Christian directs his life, an end that is not simply before him because it is always with him—the *cantus firmus* making possible all the rich polyphony of earthly existence—leading him forward and enabling him to take life in his stride. The end is the center of life: Jesus Christ the same, yesterday, today, and for ever (Heb. 13:8).

BIBLIOGRAPHY

WORKS BY BONHOEFFER

Akt und Sein: Transzendentalphilosophie und Ontologie in der systematischen Theologie. Gütersloh, 1931, 2nd ed., Munich, 1956 (*Act and Being.* New York, 1961; London, 1962).

Christology. London, 1966. *Christ the Center.* New York, 1966 (Translated from *Gesämmelte Schriften,* Band III).

"Concerning the Christian Idea of God," *The Journal of Religion,* Vol. XII, No. 2 (April 1932), pp. 177-185.

Dein Reich komme! Das Gebet der Gemeinde um Gottes Reich auf Erden. Berlin, 1933. Republished together with "Die erste Tafel: Eine Auslegung der ersten drei Gebote" (written in 1944), Hamburg, 1957 (Translated with an essay "Bonhoeffer the Man" by John D. Godsey, and a bibliography, under the title *Preface to Bonhoeffer.* Philadelphia, 1965).

Ethik. Munich, 1949 (*Ethics.* London and New York, 1955).

Das Gebetbuch der Bibel: Eine Einführung in die Psalmen. Salzuflen, 1940.

Gemeinsames Leben: Theologische Existenz heute. Munich, 1939. 8th ed., 1955 (*Life Together.* New York, 1954; London, 1955).

Gesämmelte Schriften, Bandes I-IV. Munich, 1958-61 (Selections arranged chronologically. *No Rusty Swords.* London and New York, 1965. *The Way to Freedom.* London and New York, 1966).

Nachfolge. Munich, 1937. 5th ed., 1955 (*The Cost of Discipleship.* London, 1948; New York, 1959).

Sanctorum Communio: Eine dogmatische Untersuchung zur Soziologie der Kirche. Berlin u. Frankfort/Oder, 1930. 2nd ed., Munich, 1955 (*Sanctorum Communio.* London, 1963. *The Communion of Saints.* New York, 1963).

Schöpfung und Fall: Theologische Auslegung von Genesis 1-3. Munich, 1933. 3rd ed., 1955 (*Creation and Fall.* London and New York, 1959).

Versuchung. Munich, 1953. 2nd ed., 1954 (*Temptation.* London and New York, 1955).

Widerstand und Ergebung: Briefe und Aufzeichnungen aus der Haft. Munich, 1961. 6th expanded ed., 1955 (*Letters and Papers from Prison.* London, 1953, revised and expanded ed., 1967; *Prisoner for God.* New York, 1954; republished in 1962 with the title of the London ed.).

BIOGRAPHY

The definitive biography is Eberhard Bethge's *Dietrich Bonhoeffer: Theologe—Christ—Zeitgenosse* (Munich, 1967). Useful short biographical sketches are included in several of the English-language translations of his books; see especially: the "Memoir" by G. Leibholz in *The Cost of Discipleship,* John D. Godsey's essay "Bonhoeffer the Man" in *Preface to Bonhoeffer,* and the Foreword by Bethge in *Letters and Papers from Prison.* While items in the *Gesämmelte Schriften* are grouped according to subject matter, *No Rusty Swords* and *The Way to Freedom* have arranged this material chronologically, providing notes and tables of dates interspersed between the sections. Because Bonhoeffer's life is so intimately related to his thinking, most of the works listed below contain biographical references. Ved Mehta's "Pastor Bonhoeffer" is primarily biographical.

SELECTED WORKS ON BONHOEFFER

Bethge, Eberhard, *et al. Bonhoeffer in a World Come of Age.* Philadelphia, 1968.

Ebeling, Gerhard, "The 'Non-religious Interpretation of Biblical Concepts' " and "Dietrich Bonhoeffer" in *Word and Faith.* Philadelphia, 1963.

Fuller, Reginald H., "The World Come of Age: A Second Look at Bonhoeffer," pp. 133-163 in *Conflicting Images of Man,* ed. William Nicholls. New York, 1966.

Gibbs, John, "Dietrich Bonhoeffer" in *The New Theologians: Bultmann, Bonhoeffer, Tillich, Teilhard de Chardin,* by T. G. A. Baker *et al.* London, 1964.

Godsey, John D. *The Theology of Dietrich Bonhoeffer.* London and New York, 1960.

Gould, William Blair. *The Worldly Christian—Bonhoeffer on Discipleship.* London, 1968.

Hamilton, Kenneth. *Revolt Against Heaven,* pt. 4, "A Voice Affirming Heaven." Grand Rapids, 1965.

————. *What's New in Religion?* pt. 3, "About Bonhoeffer's 'Worldly' Christianity." Grand Rapids, 1968.

Hamilton, William. *The New Essence of Christianity*. New York, 1961.

———. "Thursday's Child" and "Dietrich Bonhoeffer" in *Radical Theology and the Death of God* by Thomas J. J. Altizer and William Hamilton. Indianapolis, 1966.

Hordern, William E. *A Layman's Guide to Protestant Theology*, ch. 10, "Dietrich Bonhoeffer and Worldly Christianity." Rev. ed. New York, 1968.

Jenkins, Daniel. *Beyond Religion*. Philadelphia, 1962.

Jenkins, David. *Guide to the Debate About God*, ch. 7, "Bonhoeffer and the Mistake of Looking for Data About God." Philadelphia, 1966.

Macquarrie, John. *Twentieth-Century Religious Thought*, ch. 20, "A German Theologian (*D. Bonhoeffer*)." New York, 1963.

Marty, Martin E. (ed.). *The Place of Bonhoeffer: Problems and Possibilities in His Thought*. London and New York, 1962.

Mehta, Ved, "Pastor Bonhoeffer" in *The New Theologian*. New York, 1965.

Moltmann, Jürgen, and Jürgen Weissbach. *Two Studies in the Theology of Bonhoeffer*. New York, 1967.

Porteous, Alvin C., "Dietrich Bonhoeffer: Worldliness as a Christian Stance" in *Prophetic Voices in Contemporary Theology*. Nashville, 1966.

Phillips, John A. *Christ for Us in the Theology of Dietrich Bonhoeffer*. London and New York, 1967 (London ed. entitled *The Form of Christ in the World*).

Robertson, E. H. *Dietrich Bonhoeffer*. London and Richmond, Va., 1966.

Robinson, John A. T. *Honest To God*. Philadelphia, 1963.

Sherman, Franklin. "Dietrich Bonhoeffer" in *A Handbook of Christian Theologians*, ed. Dean G. Peerman and Martin E. Marty. Cleveland, 1965.

Smith, Ronald Gregor (ed.). *World Come of Age*. London and New York, 1966.

———. *Secular Christianity*, ch. 3, "Faith Not Religion." New York, 1966.

Zimmerman, Wolf-Dieter, and R. G. Smith (eds.). *I Knew Dietrich Bonhoeffer*. New York, 1966.